The Racing Driver

The Racing Driver

The Theory and Practice of Fast Driving

◆

DENIS JENKINSON

◆

1969
ROBERT BENTLEY, INC.
872 MASSACHUSETTS AVE., CAMBRIDGE, MASS. 02139

First published in the U.S.A. 1959

Library of Congress Catalog Card No. 59-3790
Printed in the U.S.A.

Dedicated to
The Driver over the Limit
(*may this book help him to recover*)

CONTENTS

ACKNOWLEDGMENT

I SHOULD like to acknowledge the help I have received from C. H. Bulmer, Esq., B.Sc., A. J. Burnett, Esq. and J. D. Nelms, Esq., B.Sc., M.B., B.S., in theorising upon, and in analysing, the Racing Driver. I also offer my grateful thanks to all those drivers who took me for rides, and to the numberless enthusiasts willing to "talk shop until the small hours".

D.S.J.

◆

The Author and the Publishers wish to record their grateful thanks to the following for their permission to reproduce the illustrations in this book:

Associated Press Ltd., for fig. 13; the Editor of *Autosport*, for figs. 1, 2, 9, 12, 16, 18, 21 and 35; Mr. Patrick Benjafield, for fig. 6; M. Bernard Cahier, for fig. 7; Daimler-Benz, A.G., for fig. 15; M. Yves Debraine, Lausanne, for fig. 31; M. Decoux, Spa, for fig. 4; Mr. Brian Foley, for fig. 8; the Hulton Picture Library, for figs. 33 and 34; the Keystone Press Agency Ltd., for fig. 32; Mr. Louis Klemantaski, A.I.B.P., A.R.P.S., for figs. 5 and 14; the Editor of *Motor Sport*, for fig. 19; Signor Gamberini Novello, Bologna, for fig. 17; Mr. Richmond Pike, F.R.P.S., for fig. 3.

LIST OF ILLUSTRATIONS

The numerals in parentheses in the text refer to the
figure numbers of illustrations

11

SINCE the first impression of this book was published, Mike Hawthorn, the 1958 World Champion Racing Driver, was killed in a road accident. Although he is mentioned many times in the text, it was decided to forgo alterations, for Mike Hawthorn was among the greatest racing drivers and the references to his exceptional qualities will stand as examples for all time.

INTRODUCTION

IN some ways I would rather that the title of this book was the old-fashioned one of "The Racing Motorist", for in the days when the automobile was known as the motor-car, one who motored was a motorist, and one who raced a motor-car was a racing motorist. The present-day term of "driver" covers a very wide field, for after all, the man who controls a railway engine is a driver, and should anyone be keen enough to race a railway engine, then he would presumably be a Racing Driver. As there are drivers of cranes, cattle, lorries, buses and so on, they could all come under our title of "The Racing Driver", providing they raced. For our purposes we are going to consider the Driver of a motor-car, and for Racing Driver, he or she who races a motor-car.

It should already be obvious that this is going to be a controversial book, but as the question of "who is a Racing Driver" is also a controversial subject, then I feel we are heading in the right direction. I am not going to assume that anyone who competes in a race with a motor-car or motor-cycle is a Racing Driver (far from it in fact; there are many people who practically live under our title, yet I personally do not consider them Racing Drivers). No one will argue with me if I say that Juan Manuel Fangio is a racing driver (1), or Stirling Moss, Mike Hawthorn, Jean Behra, Tony Brooks, Phil Hill or any similar character, nor will many people disagree with me when I suggest that some of the enthusiasts who race at Silverstone and other places during the summer, in club events, are Racing Drivers (2). On the other hand there are some drivers who compete in major International events,

13

even Grand Prix races, who will never become Racing Drivers as long as they live, while in some remote part of the world there may be, in fact almost certainly is, a driver of the local dustcart who has all the necessary qualities to become a World Champion.

It is these qualities, the physical and mental make-up, that this book will deal with; or in other words, I hope to try and analyse what it is that makes Fangio, Moss, Hawthorn and the others the top-grade drivers that they are, and why the keen clubman driving a borrowed Ford Anglia round the Silverstone Club circuit might also be a World Champion one day. It is not the question of having the money to buy a Lotus, or a rich father to buy a D-type, with which I am going to deal; it is more whether the driver makes the most of those advantages with which he happens to be blessed, be they the opportunities to get into fast cars, or the ability to make a slow car go quickly. I intend to look closely into some of those intriguing facets of the high-speed driver that make him do what he does, and also to look into how he does it. If this analytical study produces the desired results we should know by the end of the book exactly what physiological, as well as mental, requirements are necessary to produce a Fangio or a Moss. If that be the case, and with the assistance of my doctor friends, then we can foresee our perfect Motoracing State, in which motor racing comes before all else, agreeing to the production in a test-tube of the perfect Racing Driver—a combination of Gabriel, Segrave, Nuvolari and Fangio, all at the same time; and then the problem of winning races will be over. On the other hand, if my scientific friends get hold of the information, they may do some heavy calculations and decide that all the requirements could be produced by an intricate small black box that ticks and buzzes and computes all the known information, to control a racing car at the limit of its performance round any predetermined circuit.

Upon reflection perhaps both these alternatives would take a lot of the fun and fascination out of motor racing, as we know it today. We should all become serious-minded brains, pondering on how to make 99·999% efficiency into 100·000%, whereas at the moment it only needs someone at a gathering of enthusiasts to suggest that Moss is better than Hawthorn, or Fangio is better than both, for a lively, though sometimes misinformed, discussion to start that will while away many entertaining hours. It is an indisputable fact that anyone who wins a motor race must surely have an interesting character, and throughout this book I hope to introduce sidelights on these characters, both good and bad.

Examples and incidents will be quoted in the text to illustrate certain points, and where relevant the origin will be quoted, and the actual driver mentioned. In other cases, where the example is of an adverse nature, then the name of the driver will be omitted for obvious reasons, and I sincerely hope that anyone recognising themselves in an embarrassing situation will not take umbrage and strike me forcibly. My only excuse for quoting such examples will be in the interest of the science and art of high-speed driving, for a perfect example of what not to do is often much more valuable than a dozen examples of the correct approach to a problem. To any such drivers, I do not necessarily apologise for making use of their mistakes, but I do apologise for my habit of being in the right place at the right time, and having an eagle eye forever cast upon those who are doing, successfully or otherwise, that which I should like to be able to do myself.

There will almost certainly be occasions when I shall wander far away from the point in question, so that the text begins to bear little resemblance to the title of the chapter, but as the subject matter of my wandering will be motor racing, in some form or other, I trust that it will all be taken in good part. After all, motor racing is the real basis behind all the thoughts contained in this book, and though I may be discussing some twist in the character of a driver, he will be a driver of a racing car. I must also apologise should any of my readers be disappointed that they have seen some of the illustrations before; this is inevitable, for if a "classic" situation has occurred in the past which illustrates a particular point I am dealing with, and it has been photographed, it is almost sure to have been published in the past. I feel that the republication of a photograph is fully justified providing it is the perfect illustration of a specific action.

While indulging in a little justifying, it will not go amiss here to offer a justification for the existence of this book anyway. The easiest thing in the world is to stand on the touchline and criticise; in our case the touchline being the pit area or the edge of the road or track. In an attempt to justify the writings that follow I would point out that I am not a Grand Prix driver; I never have been, never will be, and because of what I have written I know why I shall never make a high-speed driver. However, I can still enjoy speed for its own sake, and enjoy watching those of us who are blessed with the right physical and mental make-up to become World Champions displaying the art of high-speed driving, whether I am standing on the edge of the road or sitting beside them in a two-seater sports car.

From the competition angle I have tried, and while not exactly proving to be a failure, I reached my limitations quite early on, and what is important, I think, I realised I had reached my limitations, so I stopped beating my head against a brick wall so to speak, and turned my activities elsewhere. I raced solo motor-cycles at a not very early age and, while not being successful, I did not get left behind and made steady progress until I tried my hand at Grand Prix motor-cycle racing, when I realised I had reached the limit of my two-wheeled abilities. I then passed on to being the movable ballast on three wheels (4), namely a sidecar passenger, and because I was able to enjoy the high speeds and skill of the driver without too much ability being needed on my part, I made a success of this, so much so that I earned a fairly honest living at it for five years. Passing into the motor-car racing world as a journalist, I could not resist the compulsion for competitive motoring and found my outlet in being passenger in the Mille Miglia four years running, in an ultra-fast sports car which I was quite in-

1, 2 True Racing Drivers in different categories: (*above*) Juan Fangio at the limit of tyre adhesion with a Maserati and (*below*) Jack Sears at the limit of an Austin 105's tyre adhesion. Though the overall cornering power of the two cars is vastly different, both drivers are reaching the limit. Though the high cornering speed of the Maserati naturally calls for greater skill, the basic principles of "trying hard" apply to both drivers

3,4 The author "having a bit of a go" in different spheres. *Above:* His Porsche in a slide during a hill-climb

Below: Acting as ballast on a Norton racing sidecar outfit through an 85 m.p.h. bend, with his friend the late Marcel Masuy of Brussels

capable of driving to its utmost (17). As with sidecar passengering, Mille Miglia passengering came naturally to me and proved enjoyable as well as exhilarating but, more important to me, it provided the opportunity to sit beside one of the world's best drivers and watch how he did what I would dearly love to be able to do. Finally, I have dabbled in small sprint meetings when the occasion has arisen, more to satisfy the competitive urge in me than with any hope to succeed. But I feel justified in saying that on each and every occasion I have at least tried to the utmost of the ability of my car and myself, and no one can do more than that.

Really, of course, there is no need to justify the writing of a book, for once written it is up to the public whether they buy it or not and, having made their choice, it should be no concern of the author whether they like it or not. In all my writings on motor racing matters I have always held the view that the reader does not *have* to read what I have written; if they choose to read it and then object, it is most unfortunate for them, and I am only sorry they have wasted their time. I am never sorry about what I have written. However, I hope that this book will prove instructive as well as amusing. It is in order to help you, the reader, to accept it with a slightly less jaundiced eye than might be the case that the foregoing points of justification are given.

Finally, the name of Stirling Moss will appear at frequent intervals, especially when I want to illustrate a driving technique that I have experienced. The reason for this is that I have been driven by Moss over some fifteen thousand miles, most of them at racing speeds in cars with maxima of 110 m.p.h. to 175 m.p.h. Many of my analyses have been prompted by an initial experience with this great British driver, and my investigations have gone on to other drivers, in order to confirm or deny the original ideas. At every opportunity I "cadge" rides with the top drivers, either round circuits or on the road, no matter how short the distance, for the study of their methods never fails to interest me. There are many "lesser" drivers with whom I make no attempts to have rides, and some of the reasons for this will become apparent throughout the book—while a driver of the same ability as myself, or less, invariably frightens me. Throughout the thousands of miles I have ridden with Moss I must say, quite truthfully, that I have never been frightened by him, and that in spite of having had three major crashes with him. We have often been in "interesting situations" in which I had plenty of cause to be frightened, but fortunately I was born with a critical and analytical mind, operative even in moments of extreme danger, so that seated beside Moss in such situations I found myself sitting back and watching closely to see how he was going to extricate himself.

It was the same during my years as a racing sidecar passenger. I just cannot remember an occasion when I was frightened, though I can recall many exciting moments, and when riding with World Champion Eric Oliver I used to hold on and think, "If Eric cannot sort this one out, no one will." Blind faith, you may say—well, perhaps that is so, but the fact is that over the past ten years of racing activity I have absorbed many interesting facts about the Racing Driver, whether he be on two, three or four wheels. In this book I have attempted to assemble some of that knowledge into something of value to those who aspire to being racing drivers, and also to those who, like me, enjoy the art of high-speed driving, while readers who are merely interested in motor racing in an academic sort of way will also learn something.

CHAPTER I

ART

NO doubt if I suggest that driving a car at high speed is an art, along with music, painting and literature, I should be greeted by some very cutting remarks from students of the accepted arts; but I really do consider fast driving as an art, an essentially twentieth-century art, and one demanding as much theoretical study, natural flair, learning and practice as any of the classical arts. It is an essential that the Racing Driver begins the basic training at an early age, perfects his natural ability by trial and error while he is still young enough to have dash and spirit, ripens into maturity along with experience, reaches a climax of perfection and then either stops at the peak or tapers gently downhill, so that even if his display of artistry is no longer equal to that of newcomers, the touch of the real artist is still evident. When a man has gone through all those phases, then and then only can we consider him to be a true performer in the art of high-speed driving.

I am writing here, of course, of those men who attain the highest degree of driving, the standard that puts them automatically into the first six or eight drivers in the world of motor racing. Just as "little Sophie" at the age of eight years may be quite an infant prodigy on the piano or violin, and by eighteen years have lost all interest in music, for though she may still play, her renderings are such that they are good but not to concert standards, so can a man tackle the art of driving. At first, in club races, or small events, even in rally driving, he may shine above all his rivals, but as he progresses to more difficult types of driving he may show no further ability. I am not concerned with such

21

people, nor with those who merely drive along the highways and byways in a straight line. To me they are not "Drivers", in the same way that "little Sophie" at eight or eighteen years is not a concert performer. It is the "greats" of our particular art in whom I am interested, the Chopins, the Moiseiwitches, the Kentners, the Shostakovitches. In our particular art form they are the Segraves, the Nuvolaris, the Rosemeyers of the past, or the Fangios, the Hawthorns, the Moss's, the Brooks of today.

Even though I am not concerned with an analysis of the Motorist—he who conducts his vehicle along the Highway in an orderly and Code-like manner—there is absolutely no reason at all why such a driver should not indulge in the art of driving to a perfection equal to the standard of manœuvre which he is attempting. Unfortunately this is but rarely the case, and the result is that it is common to see sloppy and untidy driving even at touring speeds, while unskilled handling of the motor-car in traffic is one of the major causes of congestion. There is a popular misconception that to drive like a racing driver means to drive at high speed, especially on the straight, and to handle the car roughly with little or no idea of what is really taking place, speed being the all-important element. If only we could all realise that speed is essentially a relative property, mastering the art of driving would be simpler. To me, driving like a racing driver covers a multitude of things other than actually going fast; it involves a correct relationship with the controls of the car, a smooth operation of them, perfect coordination of hand and foot movements, and the much more difficult co-ordination of the senses with the physical movements. Speed itself, relative road speed that is, is really of secondary importance, and if the basic art of driving is perfected a natural increase in road speed will come automatically, with much greater ease and far greater safety than before. The simple matter of driving-position, once perfected, could easily show an increase of 5 m.p.h. on the average speed for a journey, without any conscious effort of going faster. Practice at making smooth gearchanges, movements of the steering wheel or operation of the pedals, brake or clutch, together would result in a more relaxed driving method which would automatically be followed by more concentration on the road, and the result, again without conscious thought, would be a speeding up of the rate of travel. The important thing in such cases is not so much a faster passage from A to B, but the fact that it is accomplished without greater physical or mental effort, and in consequence the improvement is not accompanied by any increase in the danger factor, either to oneself or others.

I had very concrete proof of this myself in 1955 when I first began to travel as passenger to Stirling Moss. Up to then I thought I was driving well, able to travel fast in safety, without worrying my passengers, and on transcontinental trips keeping up a continuous 50 m.p.h. overall average for a day's journey of four to five hundred miles. By the middle of 1955 I had covered more than ten thousand miles sitting beside Moss, doing a job of work learning a thousand miles of Italian roads and committing them to paper, translatable into messages to be passed to him during the Mille Miglia. Quite unnoticed by me at the time was the fact that I was subconsciously absorbing the details of his driving methods, not necessarily at racing speeds, for lots of the time we never went over 85 m.p.h., being in a touring car, but I was absorbing the smooth way he drove, the flowing movements of the passage of the car, brought about by wonderful coordination between his physical and mental processes. I was continually watching how time could be saved either in traffic or on the open road, not by screaming sideways round corners and wearing out the tyres, though we did do some of this, but more by reason of subconscious looking-ahead and planning of appropriate actions a few tenths of a second earlier than I had been used to. It was also by dint of anticipating the immediate future and responding more quickly to situations and, probably more than anything, by being shown how very seldom was it necessary to reduce speed for a set of circumstances at 30 m.p.h. or 130 m.p.h., for by a sharpening of the powers of anticipation and a speeding up of one's physical movements they could be delayed for a brief moment longer. More often than not, this brief delaying of a movement, such as lifting one's foot from the accelerator or applying the brake, or even changing direction, allowed sufficient time for an impending situation to alter and allow us to travel by at unreduced speed. All these sorts of things, and many more which will no doubt materialise as this story unfolds, I was unconsciously absorbing, so that when I got back into my own car again I found I was still using the same maximum speed and cruising speed, but I was averaging 55 m.p.h. on journeys that previously I had covered at a 50 m.p.h. average, and the important thing was that I was making no conscious mental effort to go any faster. I discovered that whereas previously I was viewing the time interval of one second as being made up of five separate parts, each one allowing me to have a thought process or make a physical movement, I now felt that a second was composed of ten separate parts, and I can truly say that since my ten thousand miles of subconscious instruction my driving has improved all-round by 50%. The change was noticeable in greater relaxation, or the same relaxed condition for a higher speed, smoother movements, quicker thinking and action, greater continuity of all the factors involved in travelling along a road, a greater appreciation of the safety factors in steering and roadholding and a more "fluid" progress from A to B. Put into its simplest and most obvious form, I had discovered that a gentle Ess-bend that I was previously taking by following the border of the Ess could now be taken in a straight line, going close to the left, then the right and then left again, the result being constant-speed smooth travel, as against the previous jerky angular movement in three parts. That is a simple basic thing that we all know, and is rather akin to learning the scales in piano playing at an early age. What I experienced and have gone on experiencing and learning from since, were some of the factors involved in ultra-high speed driving. The next step, naturally enough, should have been to do these things at higher and higher speeds, but the man who does not know his personal limit of ability does not live very long, and I hope to live to a ripe old age, driving well and to my personal limits all the time, but not over them. This marked improvement in my driving technique, absorbed from the demonstration of a master of the art, was so noticeable that a friend who had not driven with me for some time remarked, "You *have* learnt to drive."

CHAPTER II

DETERMINATION

BEFORE analysing the racing driver and his actions let us consider the various motor racing activities available today, for then we shall see that one type of driver will not necessarily be suitable for them all. Generally accepted as the ultimate in racing driving are the Grand Prix events, these being for pure racing cars built to a predetermined formula but essentially cars designed with the minimum of restrictions on the designers. Grand Prix cars are usually the fastest cars used in competitions, not necessarily from the point of view of maximum speed in a straight line, but as a means of covering a racing circuit involving corners, straights and hills. In other words the Grand Prix car, because of the comparatively free hand given to the designers, represents the ultimate in motor-car potential for traversing smooth ground under all conditions. The Grand Prix car is generally considered the most difficult car to drive to the limits of its performance, because its free-design allows roadholding, steering and suspension techniques of great efficiency to be utilised which maintain a very high degree of stability, and obviously the higher this degree the closer to the ultimate will the car approach. This means that the driver has to be of a similar high standard to drive the car to its limit. To drive a Grand Prix car below its limits is not difficult, and many drivers taking part in Grand Prix racing, because of their personal limitations, never approach the limits of their cars. However, the top drivers who spend most of their lives driving to the limit of their car's ability are highly skilled when conducting a Grand Prix car, and it is their skill which interests us.

Then there is sports car racing. This is for two-seater cars built to a long list of fixed requirements and these cars are subdivided into numerous categories depending on the size of the engine. On the average racing circuit the bigger-engined cars are usually fastest, but this is not always the case and later we shall see that each course appears to have an engine capacity most suited to it. Some of the bigger sports cars are faster in respect of maximum speed than the Grand Prix cars, but because they are two-seaters and carry relatively spacious bodywork and a lot of regulation equipment they are much heavier, and in consequence lag behind in matters of acceleration, braking and cornering ability, so that their potential for covering a given stretch of winding road forming a racing circuit is not as great as that of the Grand Prix car. Because of their inferior qualities most of these cars are easier to drive to their limits simply because these limits are lower than those of the Grand Prix car. Nevertheless, some of the sports cars built specifically for racing have quite a high potential and it takes a seasoned Grand Prix driver to get the most from them. We shall see how a driver who can handle a sports car does not necessarily prove capable of handling a Grand Prix car, though it is safe to say that the reverse is not so. A good Grand Prix driver can usually drive any other type of competition car with a lower overall potential.

In this sports car group some of the smaller capacity cars can produce qualities of steering and roadholding akin to a Grand Prix car, but fail to reach the overall potential simply on matters of power for acceleration and maximum speed. Clearly, if a circuit has a 160 m.p.h. corner in it, which a Grand Prix car can take at that speed, a small sports car with a limit of 140 m.p.h. will take the corner at its maximum speed but not at the maximum possible for the corner. It may be faster round the other corners on the circuit, but the one high-speed corner puts its overall potential below that of the Grand Prix car. To reach the limit of the Grand Prix car on this fast corner would involve using a larger engine to produce the extra speed required and, as this would lead to a

27

larger and heavier car, the limits on the slower corner would probably fall below those of the Grand Prix car, putting the overall picture back where we started. We are wandering away from the driver, but the question of the design of racing cars and sports/racing cars is of vital importance to the one of a driver's abilities, and even this brief digression must surely show how complex high-performance design has become. The amount of knowledge gained over the past ten years has increased enormously and already a close relationship between the qualities of the driver and the qualities of the car are desirable for the best results and it is possible, though not yet practised fully, to interrelate the two.

While Grand Prix races are of a fixed length (at one time over three hundred miles but now only a hundred and ninety miles), sports car races vary from a few miles to nearly two thousand five hundred miles, so it will be obvious that such races call for different qualities in a driver than those required for a hundred and ninety miles race. Another type of racing is the hill-climb; these events are over short distances, varying from less than one mile to as much as fifteen miles and involve high concentration for seconds rather than minutes. In Great Britain there is a predominance of races on circuits over very short distances, and these call more for the characteristics of the hill-climb, in both driver and car, than does Grand Prix racing. The only difference between hill-climbs and our short-distance racing is that the former allow the driver to compete on his own against a stop-watch and the latter calls for direct competition against other cars and drivers. In consequence the driver characteristics for hill-climbs are not necessarily ideal for sprint racing and vice versa, but the sprint racing driver must have many of the characteristics of the Grand Prix driver. The result is a highly skilled driver but with this skill available for a short and limited period of time only. This is borne out by the fact that the large number of excellent drivers taking part in sprint races diminishes when they are required to maintain their concentrated skill over longer distances.

In very long-distance racing, up to twenty-four hours, a less concentrated ability is called for, but further qualities are needed in addition to those used in other types of racing and not every driver is suitable for long-distance racing. It can be seen that driver qualities and requirements vary as much as the design of racing cars, but this is not surprising bearing in mind the fact that the racing car has bred the racing driver, though the opposite is also true, one without the other being an impossibility. All the characteristics of drivers for the various types of racing are extremely complex.

As I have suggested, Grand Prix racing is the highest form of driving art and in general this will be the standard in investigating the racing driver, but the various specialist offshoots will also be considered.

* * * *

One of the most important things a driver should have, if he is going to have any hope of succeeding whatsoever, is what I call "the will to win". So often do I meet drivers who approach the start with a completely negative attitude, saying such things as, "Well, of course, the car is hopelessly outclassed, I haven't got a hope of getting anywhere." When they say things like that you can be sure that not only will they get nowhere, but they will make a pathetic show of doing it, in other words they will not even drive well, though they are going slowly. Without the positive approach at all times, motor racing will not only be a series of failures but they will be miserable ones at that. It amazes me how many people take a lethargic view of their motor racing, seemingly quite uninterested in getting any real personal satisfaction from what they are doing, content merely to be playing at "racers" and impressing on their friends that they could do better if only certain conditions beyond their control could be changed.

When I have been passengering the world's best on three and four wheels the philosophical approach has been easy to deal with, but when I have been left on my own I have always looked for some levelling condition in order that I

might have an objective. When I was racing solo motor-
cycles for a living, I often had occasion to ride a 350-c.c.
machine in a 500-c.c. event, by way of making up the number
and gathering in a bit more starting-money. In such cases
I used to make my objective the beating of any other 350-c.c.
machine in the race, and naturally if I ever found myself
ahead of a 500-c.c. bicycle I was truly elated, even though I
may have finished tenth out of twelve runners. I recall one
season when I was using the "guvnor's" 350-c.c. machine
for the big race, and a friend was filling-in in a similar way.
We had quite a personal feud over this, for we were both
hopeless solo riders compared with the top flight of the
"continental circus", but we had enormous battles together,
quite oblivious of the other riders who were nearly a lap
ahead of us. This attitude not only made our rides more
enjoyable but pleased the organisers, for a wheel-to-wheel
battle, no matter how slow, is always preferable to watch
to a procession. If there were some really good riders on
Velocettes against my Norton, and I knew I could beat none
of them, then I would cast around and see what other
Nortons I could beat. Always there was some way in which
a close personal battle could be fought, even though it was
never for the prizes at the top. I have competed in some
small speed trials with my standard 1½-litre sports coupé, and
while F.T.D. even in the class was out of the question, there
were always other 1½-litre cars to compete against, even
though we might all be competing in the 2-litre class. I
have been in the situation where I could not hope to beat
the T.R.2 Triumphs, but I have beaten the M.G.A's, and
though only fifth in the class, I have gained immense
satisfaction from every M.G. of the same capacity that I
have beaten.

The point of all this is more than just personal satisfaction,
it gives one an objective and by having that you naturally
try harder and go nearer the limit, even though it is only for
fifth place. I have known people say, "Oh, I haven't a
hope of beating the Triumphs", and they then don't even
try to keep up. Just why people with this defeatist attitude

ever bother to go in for competitions is quite beyond me. Again, I feel it must be purely this business of playing at being a "racer" in order to impress their friends after the event. Having, or developing, this "will to win" is most important if you are going to get any enjoyment from your motor racing, but more important is the fact that for those at the top of the tree, or approaching it, it is a definite "must", and without it they will never attain the highest points.

Fangio is a perfect example of this "will to win" and it is evident the moment he gets in a Grand Prix car. His objective when practice starts is to record the fastest practice lap, and it is during split-second battles for this honour that you are most likely to see him at his best. It does not really matter, from the race point of view, whether he is first or second on the front row, providing he is there, but the most important thing is to keep alive this very purposeful "will to win". Many people decry the wonderful Grand Prix battle that took place in the opening stages of the 1957 Le Mans race, pointing out that it was a twenty-four-hour event, and to go like maniacs from the start was asking for mechanical disaster. To me the most important thing about that event was that the drivers concerned in that opening battle, namely, Hawthorn, Moss, Collins, Behra, Brooks and Gendebien, were all Grand Prix-type drivers acting quite naturally. Their reflexes were being acted upon by this "will to win" and they were probably all quite oblivious of the fact that it was a twenty-four-hour race, or for that matter that they were driving sports cars. To them the start of a race meant the release of pent-up energies and emotions to which they normally give vent in a flat-out three-hour blind in a Grand Prix car. To expect them to readjust their reflexes and temperaments for an event like Le Mans is most unreasonable. In the Mille Miglia Moss had said before the start that he would take the first two hundred miles easily and then speed up, but in that classic 1955 race he did nothing of the sort. From the fall of the flag he was driving in a motor race, and he drove to the

limit for the conditions at all times. When he was passed
briefly by Castellotti he went even faster. The man who
can control himself enough to go slowly to start with and
then speed up later, will never speed up to a sufficient pitch
to win races. One of the failings of many drivers is their
inability to go fast immediately—they feel they have to
"play themselves in" so to speak—but while they are doing
this their rivals who can go fast from the word "go" are
way ahead and uncatchable. One of the finest examples of
this getting-off-the-mark ability is Hawthorn, and while at
one time in his career he lost the ability to keep up the pace,
he now seems to be able to do so.

To me one of the most exciting spectacles in Grand Prix
racing is the start of a race where the first corner is some way
from the grid, as at Monza for example. To see six or seven
of the world's finest drivers straining every nerve and reflex,
and using their modern Grand Prix cars to the full in order
to be first into the first corner is a truly wonderful sight, for
the winner of this brief battle is the best combination of the
human body and the machine.

*   *   *   *

During my work as a reporter on racing events I have
many opportunities to watch new drivers making their
début or drivers with some experience having a first try on a
new type or class of car, and these first impressions more
often than not give a good indication of a driver's latent
ability. As Grand Prix driving is the pinnacle in this art I
take great interest the first time I see a sports-car driver
trying a Grand Prix car. There have been many occasions
when a driver, who had built up a reputation in sports-car
racing, moved on to Grand Prix racing only to find the more
sensitive machinery rather too much for him.

Some drivers set off in a rather timid fashion, obviously a
little frightened of the Grand Prix car, and unless they have
shaken this feeling off in a few laps they seldom make much
progress. Others go off with a purposeful air about them,
out to have-a-real-go in what is to them a new and exciting

form of driving. The German driver Wolfgang von Trips and the American Phil Hill are two examples of drivers with the "will to win" and a keen desire to have-a-go in a Grand Prix car, and on their first attempts with single-seaters they both made creditable performances. Others such as Olivier Gendebien, John Fitch, Ivor Bueb and Desmond Titterington made steady drivers, safe and unspectacular, but without that sharp-edged "will to win" that is so necessary. Of course, Moss, Hawthorn and Collins all took to Grand Prix single-seaters like the proverbial ducks, and Jean Behra was also outstanding the first time he got into a Grand Prix car, while of today's drivers Tony Brooks, Phil Hill and the late Stuart Lewis-Evans proved quite phenomenal. I had the pleasure of watching these drivers make their initiation into Grand Prix cars on a continental road circuit and they reacted in the same way. They considered that they were feeling their way into this new form of driving and yet they returned lap times better than some drivers who had been racing single-seater Grand Prix cars for some time previously. That they were "playing themselves in" was shown by their very fast lap times once they had got the feel of things. They started at such a high standard with no apparent effort that the fact that they attained the top bracket of Grand Prix drivers, after only a small amount of experience, came as no surprise at all.

CHAPTER III

"TENTHS"

WHEN we start discussing driving ability it is a difficult problem to evaluate to exactly what degree of our maximum ability we have been trying. You can say you were really trying, or even trying all you knew, or conversely you were not trying at all, all of which is meant to indicate the amount of concentration and skill you were putting into the manner in which you were making your car progress along the road or round a corner. This is not really satisfactory, for although you know well what you mean, it is difficult to convey exactly to others what you mean. There is a novel way of doing this in which you give your maximum driving ability and skill a figure of 1, and then evaluate your various degrees of driving as tenths of the unit. Naturally, this method is of no interest if you are an inordinate "line-shooter", for not only will you be fooling the people to whom you are talking, but also yourself, so that the whole system becomes pointless. Should you happen, intentionally or unintentionally, to be one of this type of driver there is no need to read further, but if you can take an intelligent view of your own ability, and make an honest evaluation of your maximum ability and skill with a motor-car, then this idea might prove of interest.

The use of tenths as a valuation stems from the flying world where such figures are used in connection with cloud base in the sky and a value of ten-tenths means total coverage by cloud, whilst one-tenth means a small amount of thin cloud. A perfectly clear blue sky, a rarity in Great Britain but frequently seen from Mediterranean shores, would be zero-tenths cloud base. A similar valuation in tenths is also used in the veterinary profession for discussing lameness in horses, and a sick animal might be described as three-tenths lame by one veterinary surgeon to another.

The idea of applying this to driving ability and conditions arose between those two great rally enthusiasts, Godfrey Imhof and Holland Birkett, during a Monte Carlo Rally. They had discussed the idea beforehand, and over some easy sections of the course the one who was going to snatch a few minutes' sleep would tell the other to take over and not go over six-tenths. This, of course, was an all-in evaluation allowing for the particular car they were in, the road surface and the terrain; the variable factor of personal driving ability in their case was about equal. On another Rally Imhof was in a Sunbeam-Talbot and Birkett was following in an Allard and over some mountainous going they had a little private race. Afterwards, when questioned about how hard he had been trying Imhof replied, "Oh, about eight-tenths." It is with full acknowledgement to these two motoring enthusiasts that I now make use of their idea, in order to discuss more fully the differences between you and me and the top six drivers in Grand Prix racing.

If we can assume our ultimate driving limit to be ten-tenths, then we can say that our normal relaxed fast touring gait would represent five-tenths. Anything below five-tenths does not really interest us here, and I hope few of my readers ever spend much time below this figure. This evaluation has to be an overall one, taking into account the performance and roadholding of the car you happen to be driving, as well as your own ability, so that five-tenths motoring can represent your normal pace from A to B in an Aston Martin DB Mk III, or a Bond Minicar; it is all relative to the prevailing conditions. The Humber Hawk that is invariably in the middle of the road and will never move over is probably going along at two-tenths if you were driving it, but the owner is at four-tenths as far as he is concerned, while the pre-war Morris 8 that overtakes you while you are trying to make up your mind about the Humber is more than likely at eight-tenths. However, we get ahead of ourselves: let us assume five-tenths to be our normal pace for getting about our daily business. Then six-tenths can represent the way we drive over our local roads, which we know intimately, having learnt every twist and turn, every bump and every dodgy corner or likely place where dogs, bicycles and pedestrians appear without warning. At six-tenths on these roads we are getting along comfortably, but not in a tearing hurry. On that sunny morning, when the roads are dry and clear, and we are full of the joys of spring and we feel that motor-cars are for motoring in, not merely for conveyance, we nip through a series of our favourite bends pretty smartly and think what a fine car we are driving and how well it goes. This is seven-tenths. When we start "having a bit of a go" and begin to use the full width of the road through a fast open corner, then we are at eight-tenths, and though we are working away on the steering and using all the power of the engine we are not quite using the roadholding to its limit, so that there is still a safety factor in reserve. The next stage, nine-tenths, is very similar to the previous one, but we are now using all the available road through the corners, and in fact, on the last one we put a wheel across the grass verge—intentionally, of course! We are now "having a real go" and out to convince ourselves that the only difference between Fangio and ourselves is that he drives a Maserati. This state can begin to get dangerous, and I doubt if very many people ever reach nine-tenths on the open road, though plenty do at Silverstone Club meetings. Instead of going on to ten-tenths, the ultimate, we can slip in here a figure of nine-and-a-half-tenths, for this is the point at which most of us are about to go on to the grass verge and we frighten ourselves so much that we ease off and drop our pace to a gentlemanly seven-tenths, breathing a little harder and hoping our passenger hasn't noticed. At ten-tenths most of us are on the grass and an accident is impending. Sometimes, by a combination of luck, good fortune, a superb motor-car, and just a modicum of skill we can retreat from ten-tenths to nine-and-a-half-tenths, but conditions are still very dodgy, and the period between these two values is a fluctuating one, so that more often than not it ends up in disaster.

In a very early "Chummy" Austin Seven, with skinny back tyres and no shock-absorbers, this final state can arrive at a mere 35 m.p.h. and if we go backwards through the hedge we are unlikely to hurt ourselves, but in a Grand Prix car, a Vanwall, or a Ferrari, it might be at 165 m.p.h. and then a passage through the hedge can be very painful. A racing driver, if he is going to be considered as such, must spend all his life on the circuits at around eight-tenths; if he drops below he will get left behind, if he goes above this figure he will win, but he must bring a lot of skill into play to keep it up. Record laps are usually achieved at a constant nine-tenths, with occasional touches of nine-and-a-half, relaxation on any corner to a mere eight-tenths meaning that all hopes of a record will be lost. I have seen some inspired driving by men like Fangio, Moss, Hawthorn, Gonzalez, the late Ascari, Behra, Farina, and so on, when they have literally played around between nine-and-a-half and ten-tenths for a considerable time, and then you are seeing the art of high-speed driving as near to perfection as we know it. When you realise that the maximum figure for such people is way above the average it gives you some idea of what these drivers are like. After having been driven by Moss, Hawthorn, Behra, Collins and Musso, as well as many lesser drivers, I came to the conclusion that when they were at five-tenths, I would have been at eight-tenths. Now I do not consider myself to be a hopeless driver, nor do I reckon to be a racing driver, but I would class my driving ability as "good-average" for an enthusiastic clubman; the sort that would not get left behind in club racing, though not possessing the ability to win. If you then value this degree of ability at a ratio of eight-tenths to five-tenths for a Grand Prix driver, you will begin to get some idea of what it is like to be driven at nine-tenths by these chaps. It will also help you to appreciate just what they are doing when lap records go flying, or when they overdo things and have to take to the grass. Believe me, they are really going when that happens.

Over the years I have seen many examples of real racing drivers driving right on the limit, and occasionally over-stepping the limit. In other words, playing about in the narrow margin between nine-and-a-half-tenths and ten-tenths, and getting away with it by sheer skill. One classic example that comes to mind is the memory of Farina in 1951 with a 159 Alfa Romeo at Berne. In front of the pits was a long right-hand curve, taken at about 150 m.p.h.; it was completely blind, vision being obscured by trees, so that correct positioning long before the bend was necessary. These trees lined both sides of the road along the short straight following this curve, and led down to a sharp right-hander, taken at about 80 m.p.h. Farina was obviously trying to take the pits bend at just over nine-tenths, when halfway round the car took control for a fleeting moment, and he covered the last part of the bend and most of the succeeding straight fluctuating between nine-and-a-half and ten-tenths, arriving at the 80 m.p.h. corner 10 m.p.h. too fast, so that he had to take that one at just under ten-tenths. Watching all this from behind one of the big solid trees along the short straight I was petrified, but I was very conscious that I had seen a Master Driver at work—in fact, working overtime.

Another instance of this "limit-motoring" we shall never forget is the day in 1951 at Silverstone when Gonzalez in a $4\frac{1}{2}$-litre Ferrari beat the Alfa Romeos for the first time (5), using all the Silverstone circuit and most of the grass verge in the process. That was nine-and-a-half-tenths motoring at its very best, and he got away with it too. In recent years, in fact in 1957, Fangio did some of this type of motoring with the 250F Maserati, in particular at Rouen, Rheims and the memorable Nürburgring race. His record lap of 9 minutes 17 seconds, an average speed of over 90 m.p.h. round the fantastic Nürburgring was probably done at as close to ten-tenths as is humanly possible.

At all times when discussing driving ability and efforts in "tenths", we must not lose sight of the fact that this valuation takes into account the car that is being driven. We

5   Driving at "nine-tenths" is a perilous business: this shot of Gonzalez in a 4½-litre Ferrari at Silverstone shows him in an opposite-lock slide through a fast left-hand curve.   Getting this large and heavy 400 b.h.p. racing car into this situation at over 100 m.p.h. calls for great skill, or "speed-happiness", and Gonzalez undoubtedly had the latter

6 A top driver really in a hurry: Moss, in a DB3S Aston Martin, clipping the edge of Madgwick Corner at Goodwood and illustrating the technique of putting a front wheel across the grass with an understeering car and taking the corner in a series of front-end break-aways

must have all at some time or another had a little "dice" round a sharp corner at nine-tenths or even a bit more, but in a fairly underpowered and sluggish motor-car at less than 50 m.p.h. The Grand Prix drivers at the top of the game drive at around nine-tenths, but in a car that has sufficient power to spin its wheels on dry roads at speeds up to at least 100 m.p.h. and with a degree of road-holding and tyre adhesion that is probably 50% higher than the average sports car. Nine-tenths in a Grand Prix car is a degree of cornering that is exceedingly hard to visualise without having experienced it, and though I have never been fortunate enough to have first-hand knowledge of such cornering powers, I have experienced nine-tenths as passenger in 400-b.h.p. sports cars with road-holding of about 80% that of a good Grand Prix car, and if I was the frightening type I would have been very frightened.

Even after watching Grand Prix drivers at their limits for a number of years, and from close quarters on the edges of most of the European tracks, I still tend to break out in a cold sweat and have a tickling sensation down my spine when I see Moss, Fangio or Hawthorn dabbling around nine-and-a-half tenths and sometimes flirting with ten-tenths. Quite often during a practice session all the fast drivers will be going round at eight-tenths, neatly and tidily, placing the front wheels within an inch of the edge of the road each time, and after a while it is easy to take a blasé view of this and almost lose interest in the proceedings. Then suddenly you will notice that the approaching car is in a bit more of a slide than normal leaving the last corner and instead of coming to within the usual inch of the edge of the road, the inside front wheel now runs on to the grass verge, throwing up a little cloud of dust, and as the car passes you see the driver has a sharper look of concentration on his face and is working away at the steering wheel a little more than previously (6). This is a sure sign that he is out to put in some really fast laps, and it is time to set the stop-watch going. Sure enough, next lap round the same thing happens and the front wheel sends up another little cloud of dust, so it is quite certain now that he is out for a fastest lap. If it is possible to move across to another corner you will see the same thing. If you listen carefully you will notice that the engine revs go just a little bit higher before gearchanges are made, while the exhaust note on the overrun as downward changes are made is just that little bit harder than it has been, indicating heavier retardation.

When such a situation arises any feeling of disinterestedness leaves me instantly, for now will be revealed the true prowess of the driver concerned. The art of high-speed driving is now being demonstrated to its fullest, and if the driver happens to be one of the top names in Grand Prix racing then one's cup of pleasure as a spectator is full to overflowing. Even though I really enjoy watching such demonstrations, I must admit to having a strange feeling of fear, mingled with concern, for the driver. I can never see a "maestro" driving between nine-and-a-half tenths and ten-tenths without having to catch my breath and feel a bit sick in the stomach, for I become acutely aware that I am watching a truly brave man playing with one of the most dangerous situations that the human being has devised in its uncontrollable quest in search of mechanical development and perfection. In these days of apparent safety and security all around us, with "civilisation" blinding us into a state of almost lethargic torpor, where we have no need to indulge in anything the slightest bit risky, it is a wonderful sight to see a man, by his own choosing, do something that is really stretching the safety factor to the limit; deliberately flirting with danger for no real gain other than his own personal satisfaction. To see this happening a few feet away from me at anything up to 150 m.p.h. is a wonderful sight and I am never ashamed to admit to a distinct "prickly" feeling behind the eyes.

If the car happens to be of a new design, or new to the driver, it makes it all the more praiseworthy to my mind, for this is very definitely a case of "treading into the unknown" and anyone who does that has my greatest admiration. Many years ago this was given the very apt title of "Dicing

42

with Death", meaning that the driver was throwing dice with the Old Reaper himself, and anyone doing this deliberately is a brave man. When you realise that in any Grand Prix season there are not more than five or six drivers capable of driving to this limit with a Grand Prix car, it makes you realise that they are extremely special people. They have their counterparts in all forms of human activity; the men who climb Mount Everest, cross the Polar regions, set up flying records or submit themselves to severe physical tests, are all treading the unknown, and are truly "Dicing with Death".

Although the jet-propelled aeroplane is now almost a thing of the past, it was not so long ago that the first experimental Whittle aircraft underwent its initial flight trials. I can still recall watching a very brave man displaying the bravado of the Grand Prix driver who is at nine-and-a-half-tenths. This was a young R.A.F. flight-lieutenant who, on a cloudless summer's evening some years ago, flew the prototype jet-plane and tried the first aerobatics with this new form of propulsion. It was not known then whether a gas-turbine could be flown upside down, or at high G-forces, or whether it could be restarted at altitude if once stopped. It was long, lanky, quiet Mac who volunteered to find out, for only by trying, up in the air, could the theories be proved. I was fortunate enough to be on duty that evening and was able to watch these trials with the small group of people on the ground. The tension in that group as the little yellow and green Whittle-Jet went quiet at a height of some eight to ten thousand feet, and the ghastly suspense waiting for the whine of the turbine to restart, was horrible yet fascinating. If it did not restart Mac was going to have to jump, and all the experimental work that had gone into the plane was going to be smashed to pieces. There was also the horrible knowledge that something could go wrong and the whole plane become a burning inferno up in the air. Our relief when the high-pitched whine restarted was nothing compared to Mac's feelings, and after that it was a comparatively simple matter to try a gentle roll. After a few minutes it was obvious that nothing untoward was going to happen to the gas-turbine when aerobatics were used, and for quite a while we were entertained by some really superb flying as Mac tried every flying trick he knew, throwing the little aircraft about at every bit of nine-tenths, and as he got more and more confidence in its handling, getting closer and closer to ten-tenths and obviously enjoying every manœuvre. That was "Dicing with Death" in a big way.

Every now and then the opportunity comes up in flying, motoring and most mechanised activities, for someone to try something new, and apart from anything he might prove for the technicians, the man who volunteers for the job must derive enormous personal satisfaction, and there really is no greater prize. The first pilot to exceed Mach 1, and the one who first flew the S.R.53 gas-turbine/rocket plane and pressed the trigger that unleashed the fantastic energies of the rocket motor while flying on the jet engine, were treading into the unknown, and they are to be admired, for like the Grand Prix driver on his record lap, they are tempting fate by doing something at nine-and-a-half-tenths. The bravest of them all, who will surely be at ten-tenths, will be the first man who will ascend into outer space in a rocket, replacing the well-known Russian dog. I have no doubt whatsoever that there will be quite a queue of people lining up for that honour, and whoever is chosen will go down in history as a true pioneer, along with the first man to drive a car or fly a plane.

Returning to our Grand Prix driver when he is driving on the limit of the abilities of himself and the car, it will be interesting to look a little closer into what he is actually doing. When he cuts a front wheel into the grass on the inside of the corner he is not only making his "line" through the corner a straighter one than before, and therefore a shorter one, he is also using the change of surface to give him a different "feel" of what the front tyres are doing. By doing this he can sense more accurately how close to the limit of adhesion his front tyres are, or how far beyond the limit they are. A change of surface, even to an inferior one, will give a sensitive driver a good indication of the condition he has just left, namely the tarmac road, and allow him to anticipate the actions of the tyres when they regain the tarmac. On some circuits, the Nürburgring in particular, the roads are edged with grass banks in lots of places and the clever driver will have noticed all the points at the exits of corners where the bank is vertical and clean. Then, if he is teetering between nine-and-a-half tenths and ten-tenths on this corner, he can return to nine-and-a-half by letting the rear wheel strike the bank and thus check what seemed to be a wayward flight. This may sound brutal and rough on the car, but believe me, when a Grand Prix driver is out for the last couple of tenths of seconds, he becomes brutal and rough. The polish and finesse has to go by the board, and there is usually a trail of dust, earth and gravel all round the course after a particularly searing lap record. Naturally, there are drivers who strike banks and curbs without making lap records, but that is a different matter. It is one thing to deliberately let a car slide into an earth bank, under more or less full control, and quite a different thing to slide helplessly into the bank completely out of control. To the casual onlooker the effect may be the same, but closer scrutiny will show the difference in the force of impact and the direction of deflection afterwards. The highly skilled driver will use an earth bank to deflect him into the direction he wants to go; the unskilled driver will be more than surprised to find himself still going in any direction after a brush with a grass bank, and the reactions to these two situations will soon indicate which was deliberate and which was not.

Another little trick that is used when lap records are the aim is that of deliberately putting the car into a slide side-ways-on when approaching a corner, in order to utilise the tyre scrub to assist with the slowing-down process. This is used by many drivers and it fulfils two purposes: the first, as mentioned, is to assist braking, the second is to make amends for entering a corner at a speed too high for safety. The only way the maximum limit for a corner can be discovered

45

is to go closer and closer to it until you go over it. It is the easiest thing in the world to go way beyond the limit of speed for a given corner, and to spin round or go on to the grass, but to overstep the limit by a very tiny amount so that it is possible to regain control is to have the touch of a Master. Our top Grand Prix driver will go into a corner at a fraction over the safe maximum and, before things have developed too far and become dangerous, he will deliberately slide the car sideways and thus drop the speed to the previously known limit. The technical explanation for this is dealt with later on, but if you ever see a Grand Prix driver suddenly change his direction on the approach to a corner you can be sure of two things. Either he is out for a fast lap and is assisting braking by using tyre scrub, or he is experimenting to find the ultimate limit of cornering power of his car and has just overstepped the mark by a very small amount.

What it is that allows the top Grand Prix drivers to indulge in this sort of motoring we shall eventually deal with later in this book, but for the present I hope we have gained a little insight into the limits to which racing drivers go when they become Grand Prix winners.

CHAPTER IV

LEARNING

ONE problem that a racing driver is faced with, and which he must solve himself, is the learning of the circuit before a race takes place. A study of the ways in which drivers accomplish this part of their job shows a wide diversity of opinions and ideas, depending on the individual and also upon the circumstances. In a long-distance open-road race, such as the Mille Miglia or the Carrera-Mexicana where the circuit covered hundreds of miles, it was not an easy thing for the driver to learn the route. Unless you have the backing of a large organisation behind you it is hardly possible to do more than one or two laps of such length, though there is a school of thought that maintains that if you cannot do sufficient laps to learn the circuit it is better to do none at all and drive on reflexes, accepting conditions as they appear in sight. Such a policy would never win the Mille Miglia, of course, and is more often than not an excuse for spending any leisure time before the race in wining and dining. Even one lap of the Mille Miglia course is better than none, for at least you get an appreciation of just how monumental is the task before you.

This attitude often appears on the normal racing circuits, even short ones of a mile or two, and a driver who reckons to have learnt the circuit after five laps is really only fooling himself, and more often than not it will show up during the race, for he will improve on his times as the race goes on. On the other hand, you get the driver who covers a hundred laps of a tiny circuit, and he too is fooling himself, for if he hasn't reached the maximum possibility of himself and the car in twenty laps he will never improve. The Connaught

47

team suffered from such a driver, on a circuit of just under two miles, admittedly twisty, but possible to learn in twenty-five laps for a driver who is slow to learn. The driver in question did over seventy laps during the three days of practice, maintaining that he had to learn the circuit. His ninth lap was the fastest he ever achieved, which made the team-manager wonder what he was learning the rest of the time! He certainly wore the car out if nothing else. One attribute of a natural champion driver is an ability to learn a circuit reasonably quickly, and whether he takes five or twenty-five laps, there should be some reduction in times throughout the practice. Putting a stop-watch on a top driver when practice begins is most interesting, for you will see the times reduced by steady amounts to begin with and then as he nears his limit the reductions get smaller and smaller until he does a lap perhaps 0·2 seconds slower than the previous one, and follows with 0·2 seconds faster the next time. It is easy to see when he is reaching his limit, and invariably he knows it too and stops practising after a few laps at this safe limiting speed. Any improvements after that are usually the result of a modification to the car or an all-out effort to make best practice time of the day.

As an example of this I quote the following lap times I took at Silverstone on a damp test day, with a first-class driver trying out a Grand Prix car he had never driven before.

lap 1	–	1 min. 59·7 sec.
lap 2	–	1 min. 59·6 sec.
lap 3	–	1 min. 55·3 sec.
lap 4	–	1 min. 56·5 sec.
lap 5	–	1 min. 55·9 sec.
lap 6	–	1 min. 55·7 sec.

After that he stopped, for he had learnt sufficient for the prevailing conditions, but it is typical of the sort of thing of which a top driver is capable. Another perfect example was that of Tony Brooks when he first drove the Connaught in practice at Syracuse. It was an entirely new car to him and an entirely new circuit, though he had looked round it

48

before practice, so he knew which way the corners went. Starting at 2 min. 13 sec. he soon reduced this to 2 min. 10 sec., to be followed by 2 min. 7 sec. and, after a short break, he continued with 2 min. 6 sec. and then 2 min. 5·4 sec. He had to stop there due to circumstances not connected with the driver, but in the race he continued to learn the car and circuit and finally got down to 2 min. 0·2 sec., which he left as a lap record for the circuit. That sort of consistency made it obvious that Brooks was heading for the top flight of Grand Prix drivers, and when a year later the same car, unchanged except for having twenty-five more b.h.p., could not approach his lap time on the same circuit, and for a long time was slower than the first lap Brooks ever did, it made one realise just how good Brooks had been, for the driver a year later was reckoned to be pretty good in British circles. In three visits to the Syracuse circuit the Connaught team never had a car make a lap at anything like the speed that Brooks recorded in 1955, yet the cars had more horsepower and better handling. They had a variety of drivers but none of them were Brooks or another future champion.

A really first-class driver will co-relate his lap times, given by his mechanic each time round, with his driving style and the number of "tenths" at which he is driving, so that as the "tenths" go up the times should come down. Quite often a driver will steadily reduce his lap times until he makes a very slight mistake on one corner and he knows that no improvement will be shown on the watch, so he will then come into the pits and have a short rest before trying again. This can have a good effect on his pit staff, for watching the times gradually being reduced they will expect his final one to be fastest of all, so that when he stops at the pits they will think, "There, if he hadn't come in this lap he would have made fastest time". All the while the driver knows that he wouldn't have made fastest time, for he had overslid a bit on one of the corners out of sight of the pits and, though it was only a matter of being a few inches out in judgment, it meant lifting his foot from the accelerator and losing that vital fifth of a second. More important is the fact that the rival team were no doubt also timing him, so they are left in the dark as to whether he could have broken the lap record or not.

In passing this brings us to another point, and that is the driver who intends to come into the pits at the end of a given lap, yet goes on driving to the limit all the way round. As a "stopping" lap cannot give a good time, this really is pointless, yet time and again you see drivers do it, while there have even been drivers who have crashed on such a lap, which really is inexcusable. Certain drivers will raise their goggles after crossing the timing line for the last time during a session of practice, and this not only discourages them from going fast but also indicates to following drivers that they have stopped "dicing" and intend going into the pits at the end of the lap, which can be a great help to an overtaking driver on a twisty circuit.

Having learnt the circuit and reached a usable best practice time—the sort that he can keep up for hours on end if needs be—we then come to the final battle for best time of the day, which usually revolves round a handful of drivers. Master of this art is Fangio himself, and I have seen him many times wait until the end of practice and there is just time left for three laps. Out he will go; the first lap to weigh up the circuit and get things warm, the second lap to set a lap record and the third for slowing down to stop at the pits. The confidence with which he has done this on numerous occasions is remarkable. It is obvious that he knows full well his possibilities and that if he cannot break a lap record at a given instant there is no point in flogging round and round, for lap records do not come by chance, they are the result of concentrated effort and driving very close to the limit.

During the time when I was riding sidecar passenger for Eric Oliver, and he held the position of World Champion, we would often achieve our best lap times quite early during the practice period, so we schemed up a routine for using up the rest of the time, a routine we never told our rivals about.

This was to go out and lap at a good fast pace, but instead of taking our usual line through some of the corners we would deliberately take them on an incorrect line so that we could find out what would happen. The reason for this was that it proved useful in a race when lapping slower outfits, for if they were on the correct line through a particular corner we could often pass them by taking a wrong line. Naturally they would not be travelling at our normal speed, so by taking the wrong line through the bend we could still go through it faster than the slow man. The alternative was to wait behind the slow man until after the corner before passing, which slowed us up more than our wrong-line technique. Many of our rivals could never understand why Oliver got away from them when we began catching the tail end of the field and had to lap them. Eric would go through "traffic" as though it was not there, while many a rival had to slam on the brakes to avoid hitting a slow rider who was on his line. It was only a genius of a rider like Oliver who could get away with this, and adjusting my passenger movements to keep up with this sort of riding was terrific fun. Perhaps the most classic use we made of this was at Zandvoort when we got beaten away from the start—a thing we normally never allowed to happen. The first corner is a large 180-degree turn, quite wide and followed by a short straight. As the corner was only a few hundred yards after the start we were not travelling at the same speed as on a flying lap, and quick to realise this Eric took to the wrong line on which we had practised. Our two keenest rivals were first and second into the corner and taking it nose to tail on the normal correct line. We ran right round them, giving them such a fright that they shut off for a fraction of a second, and that allowed Eric to haul our outfit across the end of the corner and into the lead. He did admit afterwards that if they hadn't eased back on seeing us right outside them on the turn we should probably have had to take to the grass, but nevertheless it was a chance that came off, and only our "extra" practice permitted him to take that chance.

So often I see drivers, having finished practice, standing in the bar drinking or sitting round the back of the pits shooting lines on their practice times. They would become far better racing drivers if they took the trouble to walk round to some of the corners and watch how the boys on the front row of the grid are taking them. There is no easier way of realising how bad your own driving is than to watch a master at work, and who knows you might see someone worse than yourself! It is not at all an uncommon sight to see some of the world's best Grand Prix drivers spectating on the more difficult corners on some circuits, especially if the chap holding Best Time of the Day is out practising. However, this can become a game of "foxing", for if Moss should happen to see Fangio, Hawthorn, Behra and Gregory all standing on a certain corner you can be sure that he would deliberately take an unusual line on it rather than let them see any special technique he had evolved for beating them, and the same would go for any of his watchers if the positions were reversed.

Having learnt the circuit one would assume that the driver had also learnt his car, but it really is surprising how many drivers come into the pits after a long practice period and start complaining about this or that in the cockpit, or the handling, or the carburation of the car. It is not at all uncommon to watch a driver practise with something obviously wrong with the car: a shock-absorber not working, or hesitant pick-up after a slow corner, yet he goes on and on, seemingly oblivious to the condition of his car, and it is obvious that he cannot be driving at the possible maximum or he would be getting into trouble. Watch any of the really good "works" drivers and you will see them checking on various little details before setting off on a practice lap: adjustment of the rear-view mirrors, the view over the windscreen, the position of the gearlever when it is in top and third, the working of the magneto switch, the "feel" of the steering, all these vital things are given a quick check-over, often without any undue visible movement, but if you are lucky enough to be near a racing car when a top driver gets into it for the first time, it is worth watching him closely.

As he sets off on some practice laps he may spin the wheels fairly violently—not to show off, but to get the feel of the accelerator pedal movement and to weigh-up the motion of the car as the spin causes the tail to wag a bit. If anything is not quite right and if it is something that is going to hamper his driving, you can be sure he'll stop next time round. Perhaps it is for another seat cushion to raise him up or move him closer to the wheel, or he'll want the seat further back to allow more elbow movement in the hairpins, or maybe it is just a simple thing like having an air vent closed to stop the cockpit dust blowing up under his vizor but, if he does stop, you can be sure it is for some good reason. Hawthorn and Collins both had good clear analytical minds for details and were a great help to the Scuderia Ferrari in getting the cars really raceworthy. Two or three times I have seen Hawthorn try one of the other team cars, only to stop after a lap as the cockpit has proved to be too small for his huge frame. Rather than waste effort in driving the car with, for example, insufficient leg room, he will stop immediately. On one occasion Collins was practising with a special car with new rear suspension and the team-manager asked Hawthorn to try it, for purposes of comparison, but after only one lap he returned to the pits. Due to his not fitting the driving position built for the smaller Collins, the gearlever tended to be under Hawthorn's right knee when it was in second and third gears, which were often used on this particular circuit. This meant that there was a big chance of him missing a gear change and, as this prevented him driving on the limit, Hawthorn came back and pointed out the futility of him continuing to practise in that particular car. Many other drivers would have gone on and either made poor lap times due to missing gear changes, or worse still crashed the car due to over-shooting a corner in neutral having failed to select third gear.

On another occasion Hawthorn was driving a Lancia/ Ferrari fitted with a modified front suspension and steering, and after only a few laps at Monte Carlo he stopped to point out that something was wrong as he was having difficulty on the tight hairpin corners, seemingly not having sufficient steering lock. His team mates were having no trouble, so his car was inspected and it was then realised that he had a Ferrari steering box on his car, unlike the other cars which had Lancia boxes, and the Ferrari one was of a much lower ratio. Had Hawthorn not been a sensitive driver, or had he been of the type that struggles on when something is wrong, his team would never have realized the unsuitability of the Ferrari steering box. Needless to say it was changed before the next practice period.

While it is a good thing for a driver to be particular and critical in practice or testing it is not a good thing under actual racing conditions. If the car starts the race in perfect condition and then something changes during the race there is seldom time for allowing anything to be done at the pits, so the clever driver has to decide whether to carry on with the odd feeling or noise that has appeared, and perhaps only be able to hold on to third place, or whether to stop and lose all hope of a position. Some drivers can nurse an ailing car and maintain a high lap speed. Fangio is quite remarkable at this, while others slow considerably if anything is wrong, and this is one of the few failings in Moss. There are others who will stop almost as soon as anything untoward happens to the car, or like Schell who just presses on regardless of anything being wrong until there is an almighty breakage. Behra will persevere under difficulties, but if they have robbed him of a good position in the race he will tend to be hard on the car and really break it up rather than nurse it to the finish. Fangio's ability to go fast with a broken car is truly remarkable, and two classic occasions stand out: one in the Mille Miglia when he finished second in an Alfa Romeo that had a broken steering connection, and the other at Spa when he won the Belgian Grand Prix with a Maserati that had broken its front spring mountings and was sagging at the front.

Under actual racing conditions the driver's reactions to trouble with a car depend a lot on circumstances, for if he is leading and can maintain his lead even though something is broken, it is worth going on, but if he is nearly last there is little point in continuing. It would be quite a good idea if some of the "works" drivers had to pay for the repair bills, for I have so often seen wanton damage done to a sick car by a driver, either in a fit of bad temper or because he was trying to save himself a walk back to the pits. Whereas one driver will switch the engine off the moment he sees a drop in oil pressure on the gauge, due to a broken bearing or a fractured oil pipe, another will go on driving until a connecting rod breaks. The first driver will have probably saved most of the engine, while the second will have cost the owner £600 or more, and it is usually because he was trying to motor back to the pits and save himself a lonely wait on the far side of the circuit. Of course, there are some really dim drivers who never notice anything amiss, such as low oil pressure, or high water temperature, and just drive on obliviously until there is a big bang.

However, to return to practice or testing, there are drivers who continually want to alter something. No matter what the designers and mechanics do it is never quite right, and I find that these drivers seldom, if ever, are among those vying for the front row on the starting grid; in fact, they are often not even the fastest man in the team. These drivers are a real headache to the poor team manager, and I often wonder just how they ever get a place in a team, though more often than not they do not stay in it for long. You know the sort I mean—those who try the car out and then want a different rear axle ratio, or they want the tyre pressures altered, or they complain of a flat-spot in the carburation at some r.p.m. which they should never use anyway, and after a change has been made they are still not satisfied and end up with things as they were in the beginning. Even worse, of course, are the really technical drivers (or so they think). They do a few laps and then come in and tell the designer that the anti-roll bar is too stiff, or the geometry of the front end is wrong, or the de Dion tube location isn't good enough, or worse still they think the valve timing isn't correct, or the inlet pipe length is wrong

55

and so on; all fundamental stuff in the basic design of the racing car. Most designers are pretty reasonable chaps and one often sees them listening intently to a well-meaning driver who is trying to tell them their job. Why some drivers do not get a punch on the nose during practice I can never understand. I know much has been written about the great Mercedes-Benz racing team, but they really did have things well weighed-up, whatever one might think. The number of times I heard a driver suggest that something was not right and they ought to try this, or they ought to try that, only to receive the polite reply that "we have tried that and the results were . . .", turning the pages of the ever-present detailed log book of work and experiment. I have suffered this myself, for when we were doing some comfort tests in the 300SLR sports car we had trouble with a bad cross wind coming into the cockpit. I thought that a deflector between the two headrests might cure it, but they had already tried that, and had the results tabulated in the notebook carried by Uhlenhaut's right-hand man.

The real joy to a designer or team-manager is a driver like Tony Brooks or the late Stuart Lewis-Evans, for they both drove nearly as well as the World Champion himself, and they very seldom had anything to complain about. I was present on both occasions on which these two had their first try-out with a Grand Prix Connaught on a Continental road circuit which the Connaught engineers had not visited before, so that the car was prepared for the local conditions more by guess-work than anything. After the first practice run their replies to "How was it?" from the team-manager were almost the same—"Very nice, thank you, it's fine", and they had both lapped sufficiently fast to worry the opposition. When pressed for their opinions on if perhaps the gear ratios were not quite right, or the power too much at the top end, or the steering was at fault, or even whether they might like the seating arrangements altered, they both insisted, "No, really, it's fine, the car's going very well." Now I am not going to suggest that, in these particular cases, Connaughts

7 "You won't find a better one anywhere in Italy, and it's very cheap," Moss would seem to be saying to the author, who is singularly unimpressed and prefers the 4·5-litre Maserati V8 that Guerino Bertocchi (*right*) has just delivered to them at the scrutineering for the 1957 Mille Miglia. The styles of dress for this important "official" occasion also bear studying!

8 As few drivers are truly bilingual, the conversation between the many nationalities in International motor racing is more often than not done by sign language and a few "common" words. Mike Hawthorn (*left*) really believes the story he is telling Cesare Perdisa (*right*), while between them Giorgio Scarlatti doesn't understand a word and obviously doubts whether Perdisa does either

9 A designer who can drive a racing car is worth his weight in gold, and here we see Roy Salvadori (*left*) telling Peter Berthon (*right*) all about the B.R.M. car the latter has designed.   In the centre is Colin Chapman, unconvinced of Salvadori's story, having just driven the car, and about to redesign the suspension for the Bourne concern.   Chapman is one of the few racing car designers who can drive fast, and it is a moot point whether his ability as a racing driver is not better than his designing ability, but both are of an extremely high standard, so he has little need of drivers, other than as competitors

10, 11 As most drivers are incapable of reading instruments accurately, the Connaught layout (*left*) would seem over-complicated and conducive to providing false information.   The B.R.M. layout (*right*) comprising oil pressure gauge, tachometer and water temperature shows a more realistic approach to using the driver

were terribly clever and everything *was* right, for that is most unlikely, but it does show that two drivers at least are easily adaptable to local conditions and yet can still drive very fast. Other drivers under the same conditions have been seconds slower, yet have come in and complained of this being stiff to operate, or that is badly placed, or the axle ratio is wrong, or the windscreen is too big or too small. They seem to whine and worry about every little thing, and even if it is all altered for them *they still do not go any faster*. I have cited Brooks and Lewis-Evans, but don't imagine they are the only two near-perfect drivers; there *are* others, but there are also an awful lot of the whining type.

Perhaps the best friend of the designer, engineer, team-manager or mechanic is the really clued-up driver who has a sound basic engineering training, but they are as rare as World Champions. Piero Taruffi was the sort of driver with whom it must have been a pleasure to work, for apart from being extremely intelligent he is a first-class engineer and a designer of some repute, and in 1955 when he drove for Mercedes-Benz it gave me great pleasure to eavesdrop on his conversations with Uhlenhaut during a practice period. It was rather an amusing sidelight that, one being Italian and the other German, they should converse in English, in which language they are both word-perfect. Fangio is the sort of wise old bird who doesn't say much, but if he does it is brief and to the point and usually only applies to his own personal driving style, and the same can be said of Jean Behra. The Frenchman is not particularly knowledgeable on technical matters, but he does at least know what particular characteristics in design suit his driving and temperament. He may not necessarily know why he wants the car to oversteer under extreme pressure, or indeed that that is what is happening, but he does know that if he is going to drive hard he wants the rear-end to respond to his throttle movements and not the front-end; how it is to be achieved he is prepared to leave to the engineers.

All the well-known drivers have their own particular fads and fancies, some justified, some not, and by and large you

can reckon that a driver who either continually wins, or
stays with one team a long time, is not one of the troublesome ones. In these days, when being a "glamour king"
often seems to take precedence over the business of being a
racing driver, it is becoming rather rare to find one who is
capable of appreciating the true working of a racing car, or
able to make useful observations, clear and concise, that are
of some help to the designer. But this is inevitable as
soon as racing progresses from being a sport to being a
science, and that after all is what Grand Prix racing is. If
only we could breed more men like Taruffi, Uhlenhaut or
Chapman, designers who can drive as well, then racing cars
would make much more progress than they do at present (9).

While on the question of troublesome drivers I must tell
the story about a certain team who were doing exhaust
system experiments round a well-known circuit. They had
one system on the racing car that was remarkably quiet and
it was on a particularly good engine, with quite an apprecia-
able increase of power over the second car which had a
terribly noisy exhaust system. Almost without exception
all the drivers came in from driving the quiet one and said,
"It's hopeless, got no steam. It just won't go", yet they
were making faster lap speeds than on the car with the noisy
exhaust system! As this was a technical test-outing the
engineer in charge said nothing but merely made a note of
their comments, though he knew the respective lap times.
On another occasion two cars were tried out, one with some
15% less power at maximum r.p.m. than the other. This
fact was made known to the test drivers, but what they did
not know was that the engine with the lower maximum
power output had some 20% increase of power over a large
slice of the r.p.m. range in the middle of the power curve.
The drivers were convinced that they made their best lap
speeds with the car with the higher maximum power,
whereas in actual fact they were faster with the car with the
bulge in the middle of the power curve. It was exactly
what the engineers had expected and was, in fact, the reason
for the tests, for though a driver will insist that he has kept

the engine at, say 7,000 r.p.m. all the way round the circuit, he does in reality spend a lot of time around 4,500 to 5,000 r.p.m., especially when coming out of corners and he is too busy to look at the rev-counter. It was at this point that the extra power had been arranged, at the expense of some at peak r.p.m. To try and tell the average racing driver a thing like that is to call him a liar and cause a fit of temperament.

This brings us to the question of making use of the driver during testing or training, in as much as getting him to read the instruments (10, 11). I would almost go as far as to guarantee that no racing driver worthy of the name is able, or capable, of reading an instrument to an accuracy closer than about 5%, and many of them can be rated at 10%. The number of times I have heard a driver asked about a certain gauge reading, only to hear, "Oh, er, let me see, er, about there I should say; what's that, about 85, or maybe only 80"; a really useful observation to an engineer. There have been nasty-minded engineers who deliberately uncouple an instrument, such as the oil-pressure gauge, and when the car stops they ask the driver blandly what the gauge has been reading. You would be surprised how often they are given a very definite figure in reply. Of course, to tell the driver would cause an unholy row; the wise technician says nothing but makes a note to regard with suspicion all future observations from that driver.

The readings of the r.p.m. meter are all-important in the question of calculating the gear ratios to be used, and one type of instrument that is very popular is one with a second needle that is pushed round by the first and which stays at the maximum reading. While useful, this instrument can so easily be abused that in most cases it is a waste of time. If your engine has a maximum power output at 7,000 r.p.m. and after a lap or two the driver stops with 7,400 r.p.m. showing on the maximum indicator, unless he can tell you when he recorded it, it is no guide at all. If you can be sure that it was on the fast straight then you can be safe in raising the axle ratio, but if it was in second or third gear then it tells you nothing, or equally it might have been recorded on the overrun, when he was trying to stop in a hurry, using the gearbox rather viciously. The late Fergus Anderson, one of the most brilliant and intelligent of racing motor-cyclists, who rode for the "works" Guzzi team, would refuse to ride a bicycle fitted with a maximum reading needle on the rev-counter. He always maintained that if it was going to be of any use to the engineers they had got to accept his word to corroborate what the indicator said, and if they could accept his word on that they could accept his word on the readings the main needle gave anyway, without recourse to a tell-tale maximum-reading needle. Being such a shrewd and level-headed rider, he was absolutely right, and if he hadn't been so then the tell-tale needle would not tell them anything at all.

I had this trouble with a chap to whom I was riding sidecar passenger and also doing the tuning and preparation of the machine. He was quite hopeless at reading a rev-counter accurately, and a tell-tale maximum-reading needle was useless as he never remembered whether the maximum reading was in top gear on the straight, or in third gear between a couple of bends. With a motor-cycle every 100 r.p.m. is vital, so I eventually did some quiet practice in the garage on my own, moving the instrument slightly so that I could see it from the sidecar at certain points in my movements and then making allowances for the angle at which I read the needle. In this way I was able to sort out the gearing pretty well, and tell if the engine was doing its job properly. Naturally I continued to ask the rider for his observations, which he always readily gave, but if they did not tally with my readings I did not have to worry. With a solo motor-cycle or a Grand Prix car this cannot be done of course, so the driver has to be relied upon, but the number who are good at instrument observations are few indeed.

This was a problem that faced aeronautical engineers with single-seater aircraft, and in the early days of development the first step was to fit an automatic camera that photographed the instrument panel at any desired moment. If Grand Prix cars ever become really complex perhaps the designers will have to resort to the same thing.

The foregoing may sound very hard on the poor racing driver, and it is only fair to say that, from his point of view, if he is driving at his absolute limit, there is little time left to study the instruments, especially on a circuit such as Monte Carlo or Nürburgring. However, it is amazing how some of the top boys can manage a glance down at the instrument panel even though they are sliding the car through a fast bend but, if racing cars become too complicated and require a large collection of instruments, perhaps some sort of photographic recorder will have to be devised. I think it is very significant that the most complex racing car of recent years, the W196 Mercedes-Benz, had but three instruments—an r.p.m. indicator, an oil-pressure gauge and a water thermometer. This was due to complete confidence in the design and construction of the car, and I think that practically everything was known about it by the Daimler-Benz technicians long before the car arrived at a racing circuit, due to intensive and detailed test-bed work and test driving. Even the fully-equipped SLR sports car had only the three instruments. Daimler-Benz believed that, if a driver was going to use all his skill and concentration on driving, he was not going to have any time to read instruments.

CHAPTER V

STARTING

THERE are some people who think that the actual
moment of starting in a Grand Prix race is not terribly
important. "A two-hour race is seldom won by a second
or two, so why bother to get away first at the fall of the flag,
or take a chance going into the first corner in order to get the
lead?" they say. That may be true up to a point, but a
really searing getaway, beating the rest of the field into the
first corner by a number of lengths, has a wonderfully
demoralising effect on your rivals, and to discourage them
from the fall of the flag is all-important (12). I know that
when I was racing sidecar with the World Champion on three
wheels, we used to practise starts assiduously and in two
years of racing we were only beaten away about three times.
Sidecar outfits are push-started with the engine stationary,
so that there was plenty of technique to work out and we
used to practise in confined spaces such as garages, seeing
just how small we could reduce the distance covered before
the engine fired; we finally got it down to three paces. As
part of the flashing get-away technique we fitted the ignition
advance-and-retard control down near the rear wheel
spindle and, as soon as the engine fired, it was my job to put
it on to "full advance". Normally a racing motor-cycle
has the lever on the left side of the handlebars and if the
rider is going to be really skilful in slipping the clutch with
his left hand, in order to get under way with the engine well
up in the rev-range, he has little time to move the ignition
lever forward. It was only a small point, but it saved that
slight hesitation between the engine firing on its first stroke
and getting under way on full acceleration. Only by con-

tinuous practice could we be sure of keeping on top of our form and during practice, or when starting the engine for warming up, we never let a third person help us. Many a helpful onlooker was brushed sharply aside as we were about to start up in the paddock. The point of this was that at the start of a race we would have to push-start on our own, so the more we became used to it the better it was for us. I have often watched other crews starting their machines with two or more helpers, and then when the actual race came along and the rider and passenger had to do it on their own they have found it hard work and were slow off the mark. Our continual practising and improving of our technique meant that immediately after the flag fell we could gain as much as fifty yards advantage by the time the whole field was under way. I can recall many occasions when rivals have said afterwards how depressed they had become, for as soon as the race started they had not only to make up fifty yards on us, but also try to get past. Apart from being a fantastic rider, Eric Oliver was also a master at tactics and a great one for "gamesmanship" before the start of a race, on many occasions unwittingly applying psychology to a rival to demoralise him. One particular Italian rider who had a Gilera that was much faster than our Norton was always suffering from Eric's good-humoured by-play before the start of a race. This fellow knew full well that he was no match for Oliver as a rider, and his only hope was to use the superior performance of his machine. Eric would stand looking at the powerful four-cylinder motor-cycle and then turn the twist-grip throttle, getting the feel of the movement, and ask how many horsepower the engine was developing. The Italian would quote a figure that was always higher than our Norton, and Eric would then grin, wind the twist-grip wide open and say, "You'd better keep it there if you want to catch me today." Of course, the poor Italian knew just how true this was, and he also knew that he wasn't really brave enough, or skilful enough, to keep the throttle wide open, so he invariably started his races with a feeling of inferiority. When the Norton shot off into the lead at the fall of the flag it made it all the more difficult for the poor fellow. However, it was all part of the racing game and the same things happen in motor racing, for you often hear drivers playing on another driver's weakness before the start of a race. It is really all in high-spirited, excitable play, but in fact it has a far deeper effect than a lot of them realise.

There was a classic example at Naples one year when Hawthorn and Collins were in the front row in Lancia/Ferrari cars, noted for being rather tricky to get away from the start, especially over the first few yards, until the clutch was right home. Behind them in row two was that jovial Bristolian Horace Gould in his Maserati, a car that was very quick off the mark (13). Now the burly Horace had no hope of winning the race against the "works" Ferrari drivers but he was out to be first private owner behind the "works" cars at the finish. Before the race we discussed this and he made up his mind to make a really terrific start and build up enough lead over the other private owners on the opening lap to be able to maintain it for the whole race. It was the Oliver technique applied by someone not in the front rank, but the principle was exactly the same, and I encouraged him in this idea, saying, "Remember that if you can gain two hundred yards lead over Gregory, Godia, Halford and the others by the time you reach the first corner, that is two hundred yards they've got to gain on you before they can even try and beat you." From practice times he knew he could lap as fast as the others, so he went to the start really boosted up to a high pitch. Just before the engines were started up he told Hawthorn and Collins what his plan was, pointing out that he had no hope of staying in front of them after the first half-lap, but he did intend to be first into the corner after the start and down the hill, and he warned them to leave room for him to come through when the flag fell, adding as an afterthought, "If you don't I'll run right over the top of you both." Knowing that the Maserati was quicker off the mark than the Lancia/Ferraris they both said afterwards that they knew Horace was crazy

12 The start of the 1956 French Grand Prix at Rheims shows the importance of a good getaway. The late Peter Collins is seen leading the late Eugenio Castellotti, Fangio, Moss, Schell, Hawthorn and the rest of the field. The latter drivers are probably cursing for having let Collins get away, while anyone at the back of the field would seem to have already lost three hundred yards and the race has only just started

13 The start of the 1957 Naples Grand Prix when Gould, in his Maserati, forced his way between the two Lancia/Ferraris of Collins and Hawthorn, numbers 14 and 20, and by reason of this searing getaway managed to be first private-owner to finish

14 The start of the 1938 French Grand Prix, showing clearly how a driver can anticipate the start by watching for a movement of the timekeeper's right hand as he pats the back of the official with the flag. On the left is a youthful-looking Neubauer, Mercedes-Benz team-manager, who would often look over the timekeeper's shoulder and indicated to his drivers the last few seconds before the start

enough to stick to his word, so when the flag fell they diverged slightly and Wham! Horace went through and actually led the race for nearly half a lap. Naturally the "works" drivers sailed past him once they really got under way, but Horace finished the race ahead of all the other private owners as he had planned, and by about the amount he gained in that initial rush. Next morning we were all highly amused to find a photograph taken about one second after the flag fell and it clearly showed Hawthorn looking anxiously into his rear-view mirror and steering slightly to the left, and Collins steering slightly to the right, while the Maserati had its nose well between the tails of the two Scuderia Ferrari cars.

That brings us to another point in connection with starting a race and that is the simple straightforward method of cheating known as "jumping the flag". I say "cheating", but in fact it is quite legitimate, for in a start that is controlled by a man lowering a flag from full-arm stretch upwards, down to ground level, who is to say at what precise instant in the sweep of the flag is the actual start? A really clever driver can be on the move as the flag touches the ground. Due to high bottom-gear ratios, and engines needing lots of r.p.m., starts are invariably made with spinning rear wheels, and the skilful driver will set his wheels spinning while the flag is at the top of the arc so that he has grip and forward traction just as the flag reaches the bottom of its arc. As can well be imagined this calls for the most perfect finesse in the use of the clutch and throttle and it is a rare sight, but when you do see it, it is memorable. Of course, if he is on the move before the flag has really started its arc it becomes noticeable and he is liable to a penalty of one minute being added to his race time, and this has often happened, so that most drivers tend to lag slightly behind the flag movement rather than get in front of it. Quite often the starting flag is lowered by some local dignitary who has a timekeeper standing beside him, and with five seconds to go the timekeeper will poise his hand a few inches from the dignitary's back (14). When the second for starting arrives he will pat the dignitary on the back, who then lowers the flag. This of course, allows the keen-eyed driver in the front row to watch the timekeeper's hand rather than the flag, and in consequence he can anticipate the moment of starting to a nicety. If the patting hand is not visible you will often see a member of one of the teams giving his front-row drivers an anticipatory signal. I have often seen Guerino Bertocchi, the chief mechanic of Maserati, looking over the timekeeper's shoulder and ticking off the last five seconds on his fingers held up behind the starter. Neubauer, too, used to help his drivers at the start by synchronising one of his watches with the official one and, standing just "up-field" of the starter, he would indicate the last few seconds from his own watch. This split-second start is vital to those in the front row, but of little avail to the drivers behind, for if the front man doesn't start promptly there is seldom room to squeeze through, unless you happen to be on the outside. In any row other than the front one, the usual technique is to watch one of the stars out in front and, by keeping a close watch on Fangio or Moss, a lesser driver can shoot off the line with them. Some of the top drivers prefer to be in the second row on some circuits, for then you can jump the start without being too obvious. When you are on the front row every inch that you ease forward of the starting line can be seen by everyone, but if you are in the second or even the third row, you can ease gently forward until you are almost level with the tail of the front row cars. On a wide start like Monza a driver in the second or third row can often be alongside the leaders as they accelerate away.

That great racing motor-cyclist Fergus Anderson was a master at starting and it was a long time before anyone discovered his secret technique. It was to wear a stop-watch on his wrist and when the starter signalled that there were thirty seconds to go Fergus would start his stop-watch, and instead of looking at the flag he would keep an eye on the large second hand of his watch so that he knew instantaneously when the last 3/5ths of a second were ticking away, and in consequence was usually on his way while his rivals were still reacting to the first movement of the flag.

Methods of starting races vary, but a lowered flag is the usual way and it certainly permits ingenuity on the part of the competitors. In some events the starter has endeavoured to prevent "jumping" by raising the flag rather than dropping it and in some French events I have seen the starter keep the flag hidden between his legs and then as the final second ticks away he whips it up in the air. In Sweden, at their sports-car race which has a Le Mans-type start where the drivers run across to their cars, the starter has a huge board behind him in the shape of a semicircle standing on one end. Marked on it from top to bottom are the numbers 10–0, these representing the last ten seconds before the start. He stands on a platform level with the centre of the board and then takes ten seconds to lower the flag, pausing briefly at each painted number so that everyone can see the flag descending down to 3–2–1–0, and at 0 the race is on. This is a very clear and foolproof method of indicating the start and prevents any possibility of "jumping" but, having seen it in action, I am not sure I really like it, as it takes away the pleasure of seeing some very nimble brainwork on the part of the drivers. To see the top drivers jumping the start to such a nicety that the judges do not take action is to see a degree of finesse it would be difficult to equal.

There are some happy characters in racing who take a delight in jumping the start from the back row; they are not the top "works" drivers, but some of the also-rans or private owners, racing for the sheer fun of the thing. Robert Manzon was such a one, when he was racing an old four-cylinder Ferrari a few years back. On a number of occasions he would begin to drive up from the back of the grid while everyone was straining not to jump the start too obviously, during the last two seconds before the flag fell. With a happy grin on his face he would motor his Ferrari gently along and, when the flag fell, he would be alongside the second row and go rushing off with all the "works" drivers. He knew he had no hope of keeping up with them for long, but it made racing more fun for him, and he enjoyed the look of surprise on other drivers' faces who thought he was way at the back. He never got reprimanded for this action, because in the flap and furore of the start few people had eyes for other than the front row of cars, and once the leaders had turned on the power everything became a blur of exhaust and tyre smoke and the smiling Manzon was hidden.

I had a motor-cycle racing friend who used to do this, just for the hell of it. He was a struggling private owner, a good rider, but not quite in the "works" category, so there was no hope of winning, but he could reckon to be first or second of the non-factory riders. If he had had a bad time in practice, which was not unusual for him as his motor-cycles were anything but perfect, and he was at the back of the starting grid, he would start pushing long before the flag was due to fall, and in some races where there were ten or twelve rows of riders, he would be running at full gallop past the third or fourth row when the flag fell, let in his clutch and be out with the leaders on the opening laps. Occasionally one or two of the chaps at the back would moan a bit about Charlie and his starts, but he maintained that the race started at the line where the starter was standing, and in theory all riders should be on the front row, only the road width preventing this, and, of course, he was absolutely right. However, one day, at Gedinne, Charlie came unstuck. I was immediately in front of him on the starting grid and as I wheeled my Velocette past him to my position on the grid he was all set to go, having fitted his "hard" plug. I happened to notice that he had forgotten to put the plug lead back on, and was just about to point it out to him when he said, "Don't get in my way, I'm coming through before the flag falls." It was just too good to be true; I said nothing about the plug lead and hoped and prayed he would not give the bicycle a last check as he pulled it back on compression. The flag went up and Charlie came running past pushing his bicycle towards the front. Down came the flag, we all pushed off and the race was on, but not for Charlie, who was still pushing. I never saw him again until after the race, when he said, "Cor, you know what happened to me? My plug lead wasn't on at the start; can't think how I overlooked that."

It is quite surprising the number of Grand Prix drivers who never practise starts, especially with new cars, and often a driver will "hang" on the starting line and if questioned about the cause afterwards, will shamelessly admit that it was his first racing start with that particular car. There are drivers who do practise, and in fact there have been drivers who have worn out a clutch the day before a race practising starts, and though the mechanics grumble about the extra work it is better that he should do that than muff his start and get left behind.

In sports-car racing where the "Le Mans" type of start is employed there is scope for any amount of practising, for in this the drivers stand on one side of the track and the cars are in echelon on the other side. At flag-fall they run across the road, get in the car, start the engine and drive off. This sort of start is so full of pitfalls that it is not surprising that serious-minded teams, such as Aston Martin, make their drivers practise starting under the critical eye of the team-manager and a stop-watch. A slight stumble at the start of the run, or a slide when braking to a stop beside the car all wastes time, while the motion of getting in, pressing the clutch pedal, pressing the starter and accelerating away, can never be practised too much. These sorts of starts give rise to many funny stories, some true, some fiction, and the fictional ones, about drivers with gearlevers up their trouser legs, or feet caught in the steering wheel, are usually the funniest; that master of the motoring cartoon Russell Brockbank created the classic of all time with his drawing of a Le Mans start showing a line of drivers running towards a line of cars, and then showing the cars all disappearing round the first corner and one driver left at the start without a car!

At Goodwood there occurred recently a very funny incident in one of these "run-and-jump" starts. At the head of the line were Duncan Hamilton (D-type Jaguar) and the late Scott-Brown (Lister-Jaguar), and Scott-Brown's mechanic was making a big point about being certain that the two fuel-pump switches were in the "down" position before the driver went across to the other side of the track. There was still some time before the drivers took up their positions, and when Scott-Brown and his man turned their backs Duncan put the two switches up. Hearing the clicks Scott-Brown looked round, but did not see what Duncan had done and after a pause queried the switch position with his mechanic, and received very definite instructions that they should be down, not up. This little comedy happened twice more and then they caught Duncan in the act, and there was some good-hearted backchat. Eventually the signal to cross the track came and start was given, and they all ran across to their cars; Duncan leapt into his, started up, but let in the clutch too fiercely and spun round through 180 degrees, while the rest motored smartly off into the race, leaving the helpless Duncan waiting until everyone had gone so that he could turn round and set off after them. It was indeed one for the book of morals.

CHAPTER VI

"TIGER"

IN every sport or pastime, or for that matter in other activities which do not come under those headings—and I often think that motor racing doesn't—the really keen followers develop a jargon of their own, meaningless to the uninitiated but full of descriptive power to the brethren. Whether it be football or fox-hunting, cricket or cards, tennis or tippling, or motor racing or motor-cycle racing, each has its own particular vocabulary of words which seldom have a written definition and which are difficult to ascribe to any particular person. Footballers talk of "putting it in the rigging", oarsmen are heard to mutter about "catching a crab", and so on, and as far as our study is concerned motor racing and motor-cycle racing have an enormous vocabulary, many words being applicable to two or four wheels, some originating from the playing-fields of Eton and Rolls-Royce and Bentley cars, others from the East Ham Speedway and J.A.P.-engined "dirt-bikes"; but are all delightfully original, having little or no connection with the Oxford English Dictionary, yet every bit as descriptive as the best words in that great book.

A close study of this jargon reveals that the two-wheeler brigade have produced more "plums" than the four-wheelers, which is faintly surprising as most of the car world are educated to a higher standard than the general run of the motor-cycle boys. Perhaps it is because of this that the motor-cyclist coins such delightful phrases as "turning up the wick" for opening the throttle, or "full noise" for full throttle. Possibly a full and lengthy education would provide one with such a vocabulary that it would not be necessary to improvise. Be that as it may, the motor-cycle racing world has a wonderful fund of jargon to describe almost every mechanical detail of a racing machine and every move or action made in motor-cycle racing. It is one of the motor-cycle racing terms which I wish to borrow now.

The expression, consisting of only one word, but what a descriptive word, is "tiger". There is no equivalent word in motor racing but "tiger" sums up very precisely a particular characteristic of the racing driver which is not in all of them, but which is essential for a successful Grand Prix driver. The word tiger, in its zoological sense, conjures up the picture of a large and somewhat vicious beast, snarling and showing its teeth, and more often than not pouncing on some prey with its claws extended; in short, a picture of fury. Lion, leopard, panther and other members of the wilder side of the cat family, conjure up a more passive picture, either of latent force, cunning, slyness or stealth, but a tiger is essentially a fierce and furious animal. It is probably because of this that the word was brought into use in motor-cycle racing, for it is used to describe a rider racing as hard as he can go, fighting against the odds, putting everything he has into his riding, almost in desperation, in fact a sort of do-or-die effort, where more normal and sober beings would have given up. It can be used to describe the man, such as "he is a real tiger", or it can be used to describe the situation, such as "that ride of his was a real tiger", or "he can tiger".

One of the greatest tiger acts I ever witnessed was Tommy Wood riding a privately owned 350 Velocette in the Swiss Grand Prix one year. He made a good start and was amongst the "works" riders of Norton, A.J.S. and Velocette going into the first bend, and from then on he stayed with them riding a slower machine. In those days there was a certain amount of rivalry which resulted in elbowing or "cutting-up", and Wood received most of the tricks from certain of the factory riders to try and shake him off, but every little racing trick the others tried he counteracted, and it made him "tiger" all the more, whereas a lesser man would have dropped back.

15 Jean Behra in a fantastic "tiger" act on the Avus track in Berlin, when he kept his Gordini in the slipstream of the Mercedes-Benz of Kling, Fangio and Herrmann.   After a number of laps at this pace the Gordini burst its engine; it couldn't "tiger" like the driver

16 A little operatic scene including three past "tigers" of Grand Prix racing. The late Alberto Ascari (*left*) obviously holding a top note, José Froilan Gonzalez waiting to bring in the bass, and Giuseppe Farina in the middle of an aria to the "young maiden mechanic"

17 Apart from being one of the greatest days in the author's life, the 1955 Mille Miglia was also one of Stirling Moss's greatest driving feats. He averaged nearly 100 m.p.h. for more than ten hours over the everyday Italian roads between Brescia and Rome. Here the winning team of Moss/Jenkinson are seen in a beautifully "balanced" and relaxed-looking condition on one of the bends in the Apennine mountains. The front of their Mercedes-Benz shows signs of contact with some straw bales when they left the road momentarily near Pescara

It is when the racing man is provoked or up against seemingly overwhelming odds that you see "tiger", but it is surprising how few racing drivers are capable of it (15). I say capable, but perhaps that is the wrong word for I do not think it is a conscious action at all, for the circumstances are usually such that if the driver was to think about them for a moment he would stop immediately. It is essentially an automatic reflex action, which works only to certain stimuli, and a driver will either automatically "tiger" or he never will.

One of the greatest of the present day is Mike Hawthorn, and one can quote examples of seeing him "tiger" ever since his Cooper-Bristol days. Remember how he caught and passed Villoresi who was driving the big Ferrari at Boreham in the pouring rain, back in 1952? Everyone said it was a brilliant piece of driving—and so it was—but it was really "tiger"; and then the next year when he fought Fangio tooth-and-nail throughout the French Grand Prix and won; an unheard-of thing for an Englishman to do in those days. Or more recently his drive at Naples last year to recover second place after being delayed at the pits with a broken fuel pipe, and the opening laps in the British Grand Prix at Silverstone with the B.R.M.; Hawthorn "tigers" all right. And so does Stirling Moss as I know only too well, for when he left Rome in the lead of the 1955 Mille Miglia, he metaphorically spat on his hands and "tigered" for the next four hundred and fifty miles all the way back to Brescia determined, having got the lead, to hold on to it—Fangio, Taruffi, Kling, Maglioli, come who may. Recall that classic win at Aintree, when after changing Vanwalls with Brooks he restarted in sixth place, that was "tiger", and he did the same thing at Syracuse last year as well, after losing the lead through mechanical trouble. He restarted with no hope of winning, but he "tigered" in a big way, because a challenge had been thrown down, and such a driver can seldom turn his back on a direct challenge. He broke the lap record time and again, and finished third in one of his most brilliant drives. The late Archie Scott-

Brown—there was a real "tiger"; no matter what the circuit or what the car, you could almost see his fangs and claws outstretched as he raced continually on the limit. Then, of course, there is the "Old Man himself", Juan Fangio, as big a "tiger" as the rest of them when he need be. Provoke Fangio and you really see some driving. Who will ever forget his Nürburgring drive in 1957, when he caught Mike Hawthorn and Peter Collins as though they were a couple of amateurs? But equally, the last lap of that race saw Hawthorn really "tiger", for Fangio passed him by going on the inside of a left-hand bend, so that Hawthorn had to move aside, and in doing so he hit the bank. That aroused his "tiger" instincts, and he hung on to Fangio for the rest of that lap and the final one, finishing only three seconds behind, whereas he had been losing more than ten seconds a lap. Oddly enough, Italian drivers of recent years have not shown so much inclination to "tiger", though the late Alberto Ascari was a sure bet, but poor Eugenio Castellotti didn't have it in him, and Musso would not, in later years, "tiger". Way back in the mid-thirties, that "greatest" of all time in most people's estimation, Tazio Nuvolari would "tiger" at the slightest provocation and his exploits are legendary.

While being an essential quality in a driver if he is going to become a great driver, it is not the only quality nor even the most important, but without it hopes of reaching the pinnacle of driving ambition are severely hampered. Being an instinct, it is unfortunate for those drivers who cannot "tiger", but as we are gradually finding out, the qualities that make Fangio and his rivals what they are are born in them not made, though naturally they have to be developed.

You can say, if you like, that "tiger" is the reaction to bad temper, or that loss of temper stimulates a driver into "tigering", and it may be so, for there is no doubt at all that bad temper will make most drivers and riders try that little bit harder. It is not exactly a question of bad temper as one normally knows it in the human being, where he tends to lose his reason, for then his nervous system is over-stimulated so that one or more of the normal faculties become a bit out of focus. Drivers who are in a raging temper so that they are very red in the face usually lose their keen sense of judgment, or their vision becomes a bit blurred, but on the other hand they are often capable of concentrating all their muscular forces into one action, which is why they can smash doors with their bare fists, or in a mechanical activity break spanners and bolts with ease. This sort of bad temper would be useless for a racing driver and such a person would not live long, but a mild degree of this loss of temper is a good thing and if the driver's natural reaction is to concentrate his energies on one thing, and that thing is driving, then you see "tiger".

I think it is true to say that a well-balanced, placid man will never make a World Champion; he could be a brilliant driver and strategist but would lack that little bit of dash and daring that would take him to the top. I hope I am not creating a wrong impression by using the term bad temper, for don't think for a moment that drivers, the good ones especially, are a mean-minded bad-tempered lot, for that would be quite wrong. They do not lose their temper with an individual or with the car, but rather with a situation, and when all reasonable logic should say "that's it; there is nothing you can do about it", something inside of them says, "That is where you are wrong, I'll show you what can be done about it"—and then you see "tiger".

I have played second string to a "tiger" act many times, though I do not have the inherent characteristics when on my own. One such occasion was at the Swiss Grand Prix in my sidecar days with Eric Oliver, on the difficult high-speed Bremgarten circuit at Berne. We had lightened our Norton outfit down to an extremely fine limit, and one of the things we did was to reduce the petrol tank capacity to a minimum, but we over-did it as far as Berne was concerned. Tests in practice showed that, if we were going to win the race at record speed, we would run out of petrol in the last of the sixteen laps, in all probability almost within sight of the finish. We were tempted to take a chance on the fuel capacity of the tank, but then realised that during the last two laps the level in the tank would be so low that it would surge on the corners and cause the engine to run short of fuel when accelerating away. We had no other tank with us and there was no time to make one or procure one, so we devised a scheme. In the nose of the sidecar we fixed a sealed half-gallon can with a pipe running up to the main tank filler and another one fixed to the sidecar chassis. When I blew into the small tank, through one rubber tube, the petrol was forced up the other pipe into the main petrol tank. We calculated that half a gallon extra would make the race safe for us, and on the morning of the event we practised this refuelling act. While lying in the sidecar on the short straights I would blow the extra fuel up into the tank of the motor-cycle. After some test runs we were quite happy about this rather "Heath Robinson" arrangement, for it would make sure of not running out of fuel on the last lap.

Our rivals naturally found out about this and were most amused, and some doubted whether it would work, while we also mentioned the layout to one of the officials in case there was any objection to the idea, but he was quite happy about it though, like some of the other riders, he doubted its efficiency. The rules of Grand Prix motor-cycling demanded that all bicycles should use a standard fuel supplied by the organisers, and this was enforced by filling the petrol tanks twenty minutes before the race started. When we presented our Norton and asked for the main tank to be filled and the extra tank, we were horrified to have one of the judges refuse to do this. The regulations said that once the tank was full it should be sealed, this seal remaining unbroken until after the race. He maintained that he should seal the tube into which I was going to blow, but that would have meant breaking it to do our refuelling act while on the move. It was a thoroughly unreasonable refusal and there was soon a good old shouting-match in progress. After ten minutes' heated argument the Swiss judges, who obviously didn't want to see Oliver win, were adamant about disallowing our extra tank. Bearing in mind that all normal tanks must have an open breather-pipe, all we had done was to transfer our breather tube from the main tank, through the extra tank, to the tube I was going to blow into. There was quite a lot of bad language used in many different tongues during that ten minutes and, as there was now only ten minutes to go before the start of the race, Eric and I were in a pretty excitable and highly-strung state. The five-minute signal had been given and all the other competitors were warming-up on the starting line before we found a solution. There was no question but that the extra tank and all the pipes had to be ripped off, for we could not have the main tank filled until that was done. Then Rex McCandless of the Norton works team came over and said, "Leave it all to me, lads; you come into the pits on lap twelve and I'll have a gallon of fuel and a funnel ready for you."

We had no alternative, for by now there were less than three minutes to the start, so we wheeled our machine on to the grid, without our extra tank and insufficient fuel to last the race. At no time during the racing season had we ever been able to gain enough time to allow for a pit-stop for the opposition was exceedingly powerful, so the situation looked hopeless. As we waited for the final two minutes before the start we agreed that "No bloody Swiss is going to stop us winning this race." We estimated a lead of fifty seconds would be needed to allow for our stop, always assuming Rex had the precious gallon ready to slosh into the tank. That meant gaining five seconds a lap over our rivals, and practice had shown us only just over one second faster than the next man. Under normal circumstances we would have realised the impossibility of the situation, but we both had our nervous systems stimulated to a high degree, and at that moment nothing was impossible. Of all the people at that race, our rivals, our friends, the public, only a handful of people knew we were going to stop, for the whole situation had arisen so quickly that only those intimately concerned knew about it, least of all the other teams in the race. While waiting for the last few seconds before we pushed-off we decided on a drill for the stop. While Eric looked after the filler cap I would retard the ignition and select first gear ready for the restart, for we would have to stop the engine. The fact that the official seal on the tank was going to be broken was being looked after by Rex, who would have an official with him to make sure we only put in the recognised petrol— at least we hoped Rex would.

Up went the flag; five-four-three-two-one—take the strain —off and into the lead we shot. The first five laps are but a hazy memory, but I recall that Eric was at close on ten-tenths all the way round the circuit and I was determined to keep pace with his every move. His inspired riding gave *me* inspiration, so that as fast as he threw the outfit into a slide I leapt into position to keep it balanced. We strained every nerve and muscle we had; the Norton was made to give every ounce of power it possessed, the brakes were used until they were smoking. Our passage during those opening laps was sheer madness; we slid through the bends, we brushed banks, we cut the grass edges, every trick that Eric knew to save fractions of seconds was brought into play. We were "tigering" in a way I had never experienced before, or since for that matter, and I marvelled that Oliver could keep up this pace without a single mistake. Our pit signalled a steadily increasing lead of four to five seconds a lap; we were doing it—the impossible. By lap twelve we had forty-eight seconds' lead over the second team. As we approached the pits bend, normally taken at 85–90 m.p.h. Eric cut the engine, sat up and opened the tank filler and in a silence you could almost feel we shot into the pit area. There was Rex, just as he'd promised, and our planned routine went like clockwork. In went the precious petrol, and off we went again, having been stationary for exactly twelve seconds, during which time I had heard the gasp of wonderment from the grandstand as the thousands of spectators realised why we had stopped. As we accelerated away Eric looked down at me for the first time since the start of the race and stuck his tongue out. Looking back I could just see the

second, third, fourth, fifth and sixth outfits coming into
sight, "but you're too late my friends," I thought, "we've
done it, we've beaten the most impossible odds", and Eric
continued at a mere nine-tenths for the remaining four laps,
knowing that all was now secure, and we won the Swiss
Grand Prix by over a minute from the Swiss Champion.

The relief at the end of the race had us almost in tears, and
when we finally drained the tank and calculated our consumption, we would have run dry less than a mile from the
finish but for the gallon Rex got ready for us. But for
Eric's fantastic "tiger" act we would never have won, and
but for him I know I could not have kept up with the pace,
but like the true World Champion he was he could inspire
others to do impossible things. That race was "tiger".

Bull-fighting is a great sport in which to see "tiger" and
the results of bad temper to the correct degree to achieve
the seemingly impossible. It is surprising in how many ways
a first-class bull-fighter has the same mental make-up as a
first-class Grand Prix driver. Let me quote from the
autobiography of one of the great bull-fighters of recent
times. He was not quite the Fangio of the Bull-ring, but
he was certainly the Stirling Moss, and he is describing how
he got tossed by a bull, and his reactions.

"Suddenly I sensed the animal's bulk swerve into me
instead of hurtling on by. The next instant I was flung
into the air as I felt the tip of the right horn jab into my
flesh. I was momentarily stunned when I hit the ground
but then I scrambled to my feet and saw that I had a slight
wound on my thigh. The sight of the blood running down
my leg made me furious and I snatched up my *muleta* and
went back to passing the bull closer than before."*

He had been passing the bull very close and doing some
brilliant work with the *muleta*, but this tossing made him
just that tiny bit furious with himself, not with the bull,
so that he went even closer and had the crowd gasping,
watching the seemingly impossible. I have not seen the

* *My Life as a Matador* by Carlos Arruza and Barnaby Conrad,
True, August, 1957, copyright 1957 by Fawcett Publications, Inc.

greatest of all bull-fighters in the ring, but I have seen some very good ones and often I have seen a matador doing some real nine-tenths stuff with a bull and then make a slight mistake and get hurled into the air.   Usually, before the bull can attack again, the *cuadrilla* rush out to get it away from the fallen matador, but if he is not injured he will jump to his feet and in a fit of momentary bad temper, at his own mistake, will shout for them to "get out of the ring". When that happens I rub my hands together, for I know we are about to see some real "tiger" and the matador is going to show the crowd who is boss—he or the bull.

The hush that falls on the ring as the matador picks up his sword and *muleta* and advances slowly on the bull, which is standing a little way off, breathing heavily and eyeing this lonely figure in the ring, is one that must make the most bored spectator "tingle" with anticipation. Now the matador is going to pull every trick that he knows out of the bag; he is going to pass the bull so close to him that the horns will tear his costume; he is going to "play" the bull to the absolute limit, until one or other of them makes a mistake and it is obvious that this time a mistake will be fatal.   In motor racing parlance, he is going to "tiger" and will be at nine-and-a-half tenths with numerous sorties on to the border of ten-tenths.

I have seen great drivers in such a situation with a race, and also bull-fighters with a fight.   I have seen a matador killed and I have also seen a racing driver killed.   To reach the ultimate one must "Dice with Death" and often Death claims a victim, but when he does so under such circumstances let us not bewail the fact, but rather salute and admire a man who died doing his utmost in his own specialised sphere.

CHAPTER VII

"MOMENTS"

EVERYONE who aspires to being a racing driver, and who tries to achieve that ambition—or for that matter achieves it—must at sometime or another suffer an accident. The driver who never makes a mistake does not exist, while the racing driver who never has an accident is equally non-existent. It stands to reason that if you are going to delve in the relatively unknown factors of the adhesion and cornering limits of a motor-car you are going to come unstuck sometime. Unless you dabble on the boundary of disaster you can never hope to make much progress as a racing driver. The easiest way of finding out the limit of the cornering power of a given car is to take each corner a little faster than the previous one until you lose adhesion and go off the road; if you are alive to tell the tale you will know exactly the limit of the combination of that car and your ability, but as this method causes a high consumption of cars, to say nothing of the personal risks, it is not to be recommended and what most people do is to feel their way up to a point just before the limit is reached. It is probably true to say that the driver who can "feel" his way closest to the limit, without overdoing it, will be the best driver, except that the top drivers can and do "feel" their way beyond the limit for a fleeting moment and then waver along the thin dividing line between safety and danger.

Putting all this in a more simple manner, let us postulate an Aston Martin, for example, and a 130 m.p.h. corner; which is to say that under given conditions this car can take the corner at this speed without the tyres losing adhesion. If this figure is not known beforehand and you give the car to

87

a cross-section of racing drivers and let them take turns in
driving round the corner you will get a multitude of answers
as to the limit for the corner.   You will get the timid driver
who takes it at 100 m.p.h. quite convinced that he has
reached the limit; the scatter-brain who tries to take it at
140 m.p.h. and goes off on the grass; and various stages in
between.   The first two drivers give us two fairly obvious
extreme limits; we know it can be taken at more than 100
m.p.h. but we also know that it cannot be taken at 140 m.p.h.
We shall be able to find plenty of drivers to take it at
110 m.p.h., not quite so many at 120 m.p.h., fewer still at
125 m.p.h. and perhaps one or two at 128 m.p.h. and the
latter will probably suggest that they have very nearly
reached the limit.   What I call a "top-line driver" would
probably manage the corner once at a fluctuating speed
varying between 131 and 129 m.p.h. and he would give you
your limit for the conditions.   He would be most unlikely
to do it more than once, though he could probably repeat
129 m.p.h. on a number of occasions and would record
128 m.p.h. all day long.   This gives us some appreciation
of what it means to drive on the limit, and it is quite obvious
that to do so is to court disaster, but the top-line drivers
have the ability and courage to do this, though the more
they do it the more the law-of-averages suggests that on one
occasion they will teeter from 130 to 131, instead of 129
m.p.h., and then they will crash.

So we see that it is no disgrace to have an accident,
providing it happens while you are trying hard and playing
on the thin edge of disaster; to have an accident at any lower
speed would indicate lack of ability or sheer stupidity.
Apart from these accidents caused by going just over the
limit, or "overcooking it" as the racing fraternity often say,
there is also the accident caused through mechanical breakage, and once again the law-of-averages plays an important
part.   No mechanical contrivance is infallible, least of all
the highly-stressed racing car, but providing designers,
builders and mechanics do their job properly the risk of a
serious mechanical breakage is very small indeed.   However,

the more racing miles a driver covers the greater is the likelihood of him one day suffering a mechanical breakage that will cause him to have an accident, but this is an accepted part of the risk of being a racing driver and none of them gives a second thought to it. None the less the risk is there, and it is surprising how many times it happens and the driver gets away uninjured, either through good fortune or skill, the latter covering reaction subsequent to the breakage or anticipation of it occurring.

A third way in which the racing driver is exposed to accidents is by outside influences, the most common on the race track being the accident of another competitor. Once again this is the risk that you must take if you want to race. The only way of avoiding it is to restrict yourself to speed trials and hillclimbs where you compete against the watch and only one car is on the course at a time. If you are going to take part in open racing, then the risk of the "other fellow" making a mistake and you becoming involved in it is ever present. Like mechanical breakage such accidents can be lessened or avoided by reactions and anticipation. You will find that the experienced racing driver instinctively puts his fellow competitors into the "safe" or "dangerous" category, as regards driving in close company with them. Probably the greatest compliment a driver can be paid is for his rivals to say how much they enjoy a wheel-to-wheel battle, for it shows complete confidence in the other man (19). Tony Brooks once said that the thing he liked about Grand Prix racing was that you knew whom you were dealing with—he had no qualms about "dicing" with Fangio, Behra or Moss, for he was confident that they knew what they were doing. He was referring to an occasion at Monza when Fangio came up on the inside of him on a corner, and Brooks kept the Vanwall close in so that Fangio was boxed in and not able to make best use of available road space. Although Brooks only did this because he was confident that Fangio was master of the situation, it is fairly obvious that Fangio only tried such a dodgy manoeuvre because he had confidence in Brooks.

But sometimes one driver makes a slight error and, when the racing is close, it often means an accident to another driver who was really "minding his own business" so to speak. I recall a classic incident in the Italian Grand Prix of 1953 when Fangio, Farina, Ascari and Marimon were racing wheel-to-wheel, and had been for most of the race when, on the last corner, Ascari made a slight mistake and Fangio was the only one to avoid the resulting mêlée, he having been in fourth place in the queue at the time. On that occasion no one was hurt, though the cars got bent, which is described in racing parlance as a "shunt" or in French a *carambolage*—indeed there have been occasions when the scene has been rather like a railway goods yard, even to the spurts of steam from the "shunting engines".

Having convinced ourselves that the full-time racing driver is almost certainly going to suffer an accident some time in his career, let us now take a closer look at him before, during and after the accident and see how he reacts. If accidents are to be part of the scene it is as well to profit as much as we can from the results and thus possibly arm ourselves for the future. Probably one of the most classic examples of conscious thought during an accident was that provided by the Belgian driver Paul Frère, when he went too fast into a corner at a meeting in Sweden in a "Monza" Ferrari, and while the whole accident was taking place he thought what an excellent article it was going to make for his newspaper, as he is a journalist as well as a racing driver. Not all drivers are capable of such clear and concise thinking, in fact few are as articulate as Frère even when they are not having accidents. Some drivers can remember every little detail that led up to the accident, every manœuvre the car made once it had gone from his control, and can relate all the sensations including the various pains involved. Others remember nothing at all once the accident has started, and their minds become a kaleidoscope of confused sensations and thoughts, from which nothing can be gained. This is the type of driver who gets up and says, "Where am I?" The clear-thinking ones usually get up and apologise to the owner of the car, or start looking at the damage to see if they can afford the repair bill. It is an interesting fact that some people, if they are not hurt, instantly turn their attention to the damaged machine, while others walk away and never give it a thought. Many of my minor accidents have been on motor-cycles, and I have found that if I have not hurt myself my first reaction is to go to the crashed machine, lift it upright and turn the petrol off, not for fear of fire, but to avoid wastage and a mess, and I have known many others like myself. Equally I have known riders fall off their bicycles and just walk back to the pits, leaving the bicycle lying on its side. In moments like these I think one's natural instincts play a great part in determining one's actions.

One of my most amusing crashes, if you can call crashes amusing, was with Stirling Moss when practising for the Mille Miglia in a 300SL Mercedes-Benz. We were over-taking a large lorry and trailer at around 60 m.p.h. accelerat-ing hard, when a smaller lorry that had been hidden by the one we were overtaking pulled across the road in front of us. One of the front wheels of the Mercedes-Benz hit a front wheel on the lorry and we spun through 180 degrees to stop backwards in a shallow ditch, both of us quite unhurt. As is well known the 300SL had the famous "gull-wing" doors hinged at the top, which lift upwards and outwards, and as was our custom we had flicked over the safety catches before setting off. As the dust settled all round us we sat there in our coupé, discussing the accident and what we should do next, for as we were not hurt and the car was not on fire there was little need to get into a flap. The Italian populace, however, thought otherwise, and some forty or fifty people soon collected and started tugging at the door handles which, being locked, would not budge. It was quite a few seconds before we thought to look out of the car, by which time the Italians were in a frenzy in their attempts to "rescue" us. At long last we decided to get out and we released the door locks, whereupon both doors flew upwards, scattering the pressing populace in a remarkable manner.

It is interesting to reflect on the driver's reaction to this accident, for I well recall that as the lorry appeared in our vision Stirling shouted "Look out!"—I like to think as a warning to me in case I had been reading the map at the time, but more likely it was a self-preservation reflex. After the impact, and as we stopped he said, "Are you all right?" and after I had assured him I was, he then said, "What's Neubauer going to say about this one?", for only a month and a half before we had crashed an SLR Mercedes-Benz and had had an embarrassing moment telling the team-chief.

Studying drivers' natural reactions to crashes is most interesting: some spend the next few days telling everyone about it, enlarging more and more on the story, until what was quite a minor accident develops into a monumental one, while other drivers say virtually nothing afterwards. One of the calmest characters I can recall was John Fitch, the quiet New England American driver, who crashed a Cunningham at Rheims. It was on the fast right-hand sweep after the pits which is taken at around 130–140 m.p.h., and for some reason he lost control and the Cunningham ran on to the outside of the corner, striking the grass verge and then going end over end in a most spectacular flurry of bits and pieces, dust and stones, and mown grass. Fitch was wearing a retaining belt and this kept him in his seat throughout the flurry and as luck would have it the battered remains of the car finally landed on its wheels. John was quite unhurt, though somewhat dusty and dishevelled and not a little dazed. Undoing his seat belt he got out and walked back to the pits, a matter of some three or four hundred yards. By the time he reached the Cunningham pit his team were looking down the track awaiting his arrival at the completion of the lap, and were most surprised when he appeared in front of them from the opposite direction and on foot. With a rather sheepish grin John said, "I guess I've had an accident" and until the wreckage was inspected few people in the pits really believed his story, so modest was he about the whole thing.

For every driver like Fitch you get one of the opposite temperament, and one year in Sweden a rather excitable Argentinian driver in a little Osca sports car became involved in a "shunting" match with a Belgian in a Jaguar D. No one was hurt, but both cars were somewhat bent and as the incident occurred just before the pits, they both drew in to inspect the damage. The Argentinian was furious, for the Jaguar had started the mêlée, and as the two bent cars stopped he leapt out of the Osca, his face purple with rage, and ran back to the Jaguar pit and did his best to punch the poor frightened Belgian on the nose. As the incident had occurred just out of sight of those of us in the pit area it was a most comic scene to watch, for at first there seemed no reason for the excitement, or for either of them to stop at all, but then hearing the abuse being hurled in all directions and seeing that both cars were bent, things became a little clearer.

It is perhaps the wide range of temperaments and characters with which racing, especially International racing, is filled that makes it such an amusing "circus" (16). It often develops into an absolute pantomime, but I am glad to say that seldom if ever do fits of temperament and shouting and yelling last for long.

In one race where I was riding sidecar passenger to a Belgian rider, in fact it was in a National Belgian race, we were battling for the lead with another sidecar outfit, both of us on flat-twin B.M.W. machines. It was a close race and there was a certain amount of what I refer to as "pushing and shoving" going on; in other words, neither rider was the superior and it was a pretty free-for-all dice. Having got the lead on a hairpin bend my rider was determined to keep it on the next fast left-hand bend, but the other chap was equally determined. It so happened that we were riding with a sidecar on the right and the other fellow had his on the left and in trying to go by on the inside of the corner his right-hand cylinder head struck our left-hand one and broke the carburetter clean off! As we came to rest firing on one cylinder, the other one's carburetter hanging by the petrol pipe, and our rival disappeared into the middle distance, I thought my Belgian friend was going to throw a fit. The whole thing had been decidedly dodgy and by rights we should have been suffering from acute fright, but in fact we didn't think how near we had been to the two outfits looping-the-loop until long afterwards. My pal played hell the whole time that we spent in walking back to the pits, and when we arrived the race was over and our rival was just collecting his bouquet of flowers. This really infuriated Marcel, and before I could stop him he had rushed up to the winner and knocked him flat on his back. Up jumped the other chap, the flowers and spectators scattered around, and the two of them set to and had a terrific scrap until their respective wives prevailed upon the bystanders to intervene and stop them. It was all good clean fun, and after letting off steam the whole incident was forgotten and we had many more races against each other after that, with no hard feelings. In those days one could almost be sure of some light entertainment among the riders when the racing got dull.

To go further in the question of crashes, a driver who can remain calm can often minimize the dangers, for if he is on top of the situation he can take a certain amount of avoiding action, especially if the impact is some time in arriving. Colin Chapman told me after his crash at Rheims, on the only occasion he drove a Vanwall, that he had plenty of time to see the crash coming. It will be recalled that he arrived at Thillois hairpin too fast, had a brake lock and so lost all steering reaction, and rammed Hawthorn's Vanwall in the tail. Chapman said that as soon as he realised he was going to ram the other Vanwall he let go of the steering wheel and put his hands on the scuttle, bracing himself for the impact. This action certainly saved him from smashing his face on the steering wheel, for the wheel itself would have bent or broken under the impact. Going back into the past, there is that classic occasion when the late Fred Dixon literally flew over a hedge in his Riley during the Ulster T.T. Realising a big crash was rapidly approaching Dixon switched

18, 19 In Grand Prix racing situations often become a little tense, if not actually dangerous. *Above:* Masten Gregory is seen at rest after "over-cooking it" on the Thillois hairpin at Rheims, having come from the left of the picture. The unconcerned air of the late Luigi Musso, who is passing, is typical of the way Grand Prix drivers must react to finding someone spinning in their path. *Below:* The late Felice Bonetto in a Maserati rubbing wheels with Piero Taruffi's Ferrari shows a good example of the "pushin' and shovin'" that goes on when the racing gets close. The incident resolved into a mild bumping with no serious consequences

20 Due to complete front-end break-away on wet roads, Stirling Moss, with the author as passenger, went over the edge of a mountainside during the 1956 Mille Miglia, in this Maserati. After getting out unscathed and seeing the tree which had stopped them from careering down the hillside for another three hundred feet the author should have been frightened, but he felt it was then too late and not worth while!

21 The limiting factors of the perfect driver are anticipation and judgment. Here Fangio is seen in a very crumpled 3-litre sports Maserati after having made an error of judgment. His other faculties probably saved him from injury and also minimised the damage, so that he was able to continue to drive the car

off the ignition while the car was actually in mid-air, and a photographer recorded the moment for posterity.

This ability to remain in control of all your faculties when the unexpected happens can not only minimize the injury but can also be used to avoid accidents at times, and this brings us to a most interesting faculty in the human animal which is not peculiar to racing drivers, in fact it is not really essential for a good driver, but if he has it then he will find life a lot simpler, especially when he "overcooks things" and gets into difficulties (18). This quality is his sense of position in space. We all have this sensitivity, but in some people it is much stronger than in others. In our nervous system we have parts known as receptors, these being specialised cells which are very sensitive to outside stimuli, and those which are stimulated by the movement and position of the body as a whole, or of parts of the body, are termed proprioceptors. The proprioceptive system includes parts of the inner ear, and also many receptors in muscles, tendons and joints which tell us which muscles are being used and to what extent. Then, deep in the bone of the skull and lying next to the ultimate organ of hearing, are the fluid-filled proprioceptive parts of the inner ear; one for telling us our static position with respect to gravity and the other (the semi-circular canals) responding to movements in any plane. On each side the canals are three in number, all at right angles to each other, and when any acceleration occurs the fluid of one or more canals lags behind due to its inertia. There are sensitive areas in each canal which inform the brain of the movement occurring in their own canal and, from this information, the direction and magnitude of the linear or angular acceleration can be perceived. Exactly the same happens in deceleration, of course. The other great receptors for information on our position in space are the eyes, which is why we do not feel so stable if we move with our eyes closed or in total darkness. The responses generated by both visual and proprioceptive stimuli are usually unconscious, i.e. truly reflex, and usually consist of small righting movements to maintain equilibrium during any action, and even whilst standing still since the erect human is an unstable object. It is of course possible to be consciously aware of one's position and this is done by breaking into the receptor side of the reflex arcs: the accuracy of the information varies from person to person and from time to time, and depends on the sensitivity of the visual and proprioceptive receptors and the accuracy of integration of their information in the brain. Likewise, other things being equal, the accuracy and control of our movements depend on the same things. Some people become unstable at a relatively small movement of their body from a normal position, while others show remarkable control of their body no matter in what position it may be.

Examples of human beings in whom this power is particularly well developed are ballet dancers, who will perform a spin in mid-air and always land in the right position and direction, ice-skaters and trapeze artists; the latter are probably the most advanced examples. As the artist swings from one trapeze to another, changing direction in mid-air, his senses are working overtime to keep his brain fully informed of every instant of movement. The bull-fighter, when he places the *banderillas* and spins his body out of the way of the deadly horns, or the skier in a *slalom*, the acrobatic high diver, the stunt-flyer, they must all have extremely sensitive proprioceptors, and so must our racing driver when he loses control and spins round, that is if he hopes to avoid having accidents, or wants to get himself out of difficult situations. We have all seen a driver have a wild slide that develops into a spin and he then gets out of it and keeps going the way he originally intended. Such an action usually calls forth cries of "Well driven" or "Well held", but the cries should be for "excellent proprioception", for driving has little to do with it at the critical point. Equally we have all seen the driver who spins helplessly and ends up not knowing whether he is coming or going—bad proprioception.

I recently saw a film of a Ferrari sports car getting into a spin at Tertre Rouge on the Le Mans circuit and by sheer luck it stayed on the road, but you could see that the driver had given up all hope of regaining control. The car's final movements were slow and leisurely and it literally rolled across the road backwards, the driver doing nothing to regain control. Clearly he had become confused and had no idea of his position or direction of travel. Further, he did not react in any way but sat in the car transfixed while it rolled to a stop in the middle of the road. This shows that the confusion extended down to his unconscious reflex levels and marks him as a rather dangerous racing driver who is unlikely to reach the top, for a driver better equipped with positional senses would have kept pace with the evolutions of the car and at the right moment regained control and driven off.

On the other hand, while actually at Le Mans during practice I saw Edgar Barth lose adhesion on the rear-wheels of the "works" Porsche Spyder at 140 m.p.h., just at the exit of a full-bore right-hand curve. The car spun down the centre of the road, passing me as it did so, and completed eight revolutions before coming to rest. Its final half-revolution was finishing with the car at right angles to the direction of travel; the driver selected bottom gear as the nose of the car swung round towards the way he had been going, and he let in the clutch and carried on seemingly unconcerned. He no doubt had his fright reactions when he got back to the pits! The important thing was that his vision and proprioceptors were keeping him informed of his position relative to the normal, so that he could choose the correct moment to take action.

Another example of seeing a driver with excellent proprioception in action was at Spa some years back when Maurice Trintignant borrowed a Ferrari for a few laps practice. He was going up the climbing sweep of l'Eau Rouge bend when the rear wheels lost adhesion and he spun through two complete revolutions at some 70 m.p.h., and through the final 90 degrees the car had almost lost all forward momentum. Trintignant had stalled the engine on the first spin, but as the car reached the end of its movement he realised that it was going to finish up pointing in the original direction of travel, and also slap in the middle of the road. As the nose of the car slid round to complete the second 360-degree turn he banged the gearlever into bottom, took his foot off the clutch, started the engine and drove on. Watching this it was not obvious that he had restarted the engine or moved the gearlever, for it all happened in a very short space of time, and I was quite a distance away, but afterwards I talked to him about the incident and he recounted the whole movement of the car from beginning to end, and described exactly the moment when he realised that he could restart the engine and carry on the way he had been going.

This is the sort of incident that is often described as "presence of mind" but in fact it depends on the accurate receiving and understanding of positional information; and well-coordinated muscular responses resulting from these.

It is doubtful whether any driver ever consciously practises these faculties, but possessors of good proprioception are not rare by any means; in fact, most people are quite well-equipped and the ability is shown in various activities such as diving, springboard jumping, gymnastics or skiing, so that racing drivers who indulge in these activities when they are not racing are actually keeping more than just physically healthy, they are keeping their positional senses stimulated and sharpened. Personally I have found that my own proprioceptors are of a quite high order and on the numerous occasions when I have got into a spin in a car, or on a sidecar outfit, I have known at all times exactly what my progress has been. On the other hand you meet drivers who spin and yet have no idea at all whether they revolved six times or only once, their minds seemingly going blank the moment they get beyond a certain angular velocity. Having good positional senses makes life a lot easier when you are a passenger at racing speeds, for though the chances of furious spinning are probably low, there is every opportunity for taking a corner in a full-lock slide, either deliberately or by mistake, and it is then an easy matter to observe every

detailed movement of the car and anticipate its next instantaneous movement. This avoids being taken into the
unknown, and it prevents fright occurring.

A friend of mine was with me when I arrived at a corner
much too fast in the dark one night and we slid through 90
degrees, hit the near-side earth bank, and flicked the tail to
90 degrees the other way, then hit the bank on the off-side.
By that time I had got into step on the steering, so that after
one more slide to the left I got the car straight. During all
this wheel winding and direction changing I had knocked the
lights switch off, but we carried on unharmed into inky
blackness until I put the lights on again. Meanwhile my
friend had been sitting happily observing the motions of the
car, its reactions to my efforts on the steering wheel, and the
distance we were travelling while the directional changes
were taking place. He found it most absorbing and instructive, and instead of panicking during that second or
two he profited greatly from the experience. Personally I
recall that I had been far too busy putting on lock, taking it
off and putting it on again, in my endeavours to catch up
with the antics of the car, to pay much heed to our actual
movements, but I have been in the same situation as he was
and found that I too could sit detached and observe the
happenings with an analytical mind.

When travelling from Oxford to London as passenger in
a Citröen on one occasion, we were approaching the Lambert
Arms Hotel when a drophead Jaguar drove slowly across the
road in front of us without lights. It was raining and we
did not see it until it was in our headlights, and my driver
put on left lock and braked, which immediately put us into
a 180-degree slide from our side of the road diagonally
across to the right-hand side, fortunately behind the Jaguar.
At this point in the road there is a wide gravel verge in front
of the hotel and we slid backwards on to this gravel, and I
recollect quite clearly looking in through the lighted windows
of the hotel as we travelled past them going backwards. My
companion called the Jaguar driver some very abusive names,
apologised to me for letting the incident happen, and drove

off after the Jaguar that had not even stopped, its driver being oblivious to the accident he had nearly caused.

If the driver can maintain his sense of position in the early part of a skid he can often resolve the situation by what would normally be the wrong action. On a number of occasions I have got myself into slides that would have ended up by hitting the bank or going into a ditch, but thanks to this aptitude, plus of course a knowledge of driving and cars and their reactions, I have got away unscathed. On one occasion I rounded a right-hand curve at about 50 m.p.h. on a wet road to find a policeman in front of me with his hand raised. It was in the country and an accident had happened, so he was trying to stop me running into the wreckage. Having to apply the brakes in the corner put the rear wheels into a slide and I automatically put on opposite lock. It soon became obvious that a number of undesirable things were about to happen; the tail of the car was swinging round in an arc faster than the steering could correct and the locked wheels were not helping stability. I could see that if I maintained the *status quo* I was going to slide gracefully round through 180 degrees and finish up in the right-hand ditch. Thanks to being in full command of my position in space, I let the brakes off when I was at 90 degrees to the direction of the road and unwound the steering from full left lock to full right lock, at the same time pressing the accelerator. This had the effect of flicking the tail of the car to complete the 180-degree turn almost instantaneously and before I reached the edge of the road. I was now on the opposite side of the road from where I started and pointing in the opposite direction, so I went home another way. I felt it would be impossible to explain proprioception, reflexes and oversteer to a bucolic constable, who by this time was looking a little worried.

Motoring through Sicily in open mountain country I was sliding my Porsche through a long series of bends, on each successive one getting the rear wheels more and more out of line with the front ones, until I finally overdid it and again, by spinning the steering on to full opposite lock and applying power, I was able to put the car into a 180-degree flick-turn and stop without going off the road. Naturally, one must have an acute sense of mechanical "feel" to know the exact moment at which to take action and how much steering and throttle to apply, but unless the basic senses we have discussed are in full command of the situation you will lose your sense of position, the slide develops and then nothing will help you. Every time there is a light fall of snow I take my car to a near-by open space, actually an army parade ground, and while no one is looking I practise this spin action and keep my integration and muscular coordination sharpened. I also find a motor-cycle and sidecar are ideal for practising this in snow, and it is possible to do a flick-turn through 180-degrees without using more than half the road.

This is the sort of thing I put under the heading of advanced driving as training for motoring at high "tenth values". I will not use the term high-speed driving, for that conjures up rushing along a straight road at 100 m.p.h. As we have seen, you can be at a high "tenths value" without going over 50 m.p.h., and an accurate sense of instantaneous position in space is a great aid to safety as the "tenths" increase.

CHAPTER VIII

FRIGHT

I SUPPOSE everyone at some time or another has suffered from acute fright; that state in which you can feel your complexion turning very pale and you then begin to perspire and your heart beats much faster. Such a condition is brought about by the brain suddenly receiving information that is entirely new or unexpected, in fact, the "unknown quantity"; and all the human instincts prepare to defend themselves against it. This is the simple reason why some people are frightened of the dark; they have been relying too much on their visual senses to feed them with information about their surroundings, and a complete cessation of this information being fed to the brain through the eyes puts them in a frightened condition. If they can quickly bring into play their other senses, of feel, smell and hearing, then the darkness holds no fear for them. A blind man, for example, will not be afraid of the dark, for his other senses have been sharpened to above average to deal with his particular situation. By experience we can make ourselves deal with conditions of total darkness, as for example when we enter a familiar room at night and make our way across it to find the light switch. Providing the room has not been changed since we last saw it our memory can guide us to the switch. While doing this, our anticipation is also at work, preparing us for a chair having been moved, a table turned round, or even the cat being asleep on the floor, and if we bump into any of these things we know immediately what has happened. Our anticipation was preparing us, and our other senses confirmed, but if there is something in the room that we do not recognise and were not anticipating,

104

then we are liable to suffer from an attack of fright until we can deduce what the unknown object is. This is best explained as a process of integration in the brain whereby the various sensory inputs are correlated with experience. If the resulting pattern is familiar recognition follows; if not, perplexity and fear are the outcome.

Now, it is easy to appreciate that the greater our experience and the more developed our natural senses, the less is the probability of our being frightened. Young children frighten easily on receiving new unknown knowledge that they cannot put into any of their limited categories, while babies do not frighten while they are in a new-born state as they have no experience, so that known and unknown are one and the same thing. Old people can frighten easily either due to losing the full use of one of their senses or because they are unable to remember past experiences. The average human being who is fully developed, with wide experience, does not frighten easily, but the narrow-minded person does; the same applies to our Racing Drivers. It is not possible for a human being never to be frightened, for that would mean he had an explanation for everything; but it is true that some people, by using a combination of experience, knowledge, anticipation and sharp senses, do not frighten very easily.

People often ask me if I am frightened when being driven at 170 m.p.h. or at nine-tenths by Stirling Moss, but I always point out that if I was I would not allow it to happen. Due to a long and intensive study of motoring and motor racing there is little that I cannot put into some category of previous experience or knowledge, providing—and this is important—that I can be in a position to anticipate probabilities. I have been momentarily frightened when I have been a passenger at high speed on a road I know well but when I have not been looking forward. I can recall occasions when, knowing the road was straight for some miles, I have studied a map or made some notes at 130 m.p.h. and my sense of anticipation has suggested that the car will remain under the present conditions for perhaps a minute and a half. If after one minute the driver brakes really hard, I find I suffer a small inward feeling of fright until I can re-adjust my senses to the changed conditions—by looking up from my map to see why the brakes are hard on. As soon as the obstruction to our progress is seen, the knowledge is immediately sorted into compartments of the brain, and providing nothing is left over the fright disappears. This is an example of the unknown causing me fright, but had I been watching the road there would have been no unknown and fright would not have occurred.

An interesting sidelight on this happened one day when I was driving and Moss was passenger and, as I had blown a fuse on the horn circuit, he was crouched under the scuttle fitting a new fuse by way of relieving the boredom of being driven at 80 m.p.h. by me. A horse and cart appeared in our path and, while it was not a dangerous situation, I had to stand very firmly on the brake pedal. As we were screeching to a stop I heard a calm voice from under the scuttle say, "Are we going to hit it, Denis?" It made me realise that his sense of anticipation was extremely sharp and was still acting on the road conditions even though his mind was occupied with mending a fuse. However, later on I frightened Stirling by falling out of bed during a lurid dream, and in doing so I knocked over a table, lamp and telephone. He was sound asleep in the next bed at the time and the crash of falling furniture at 3 a.m. woke him. When I picked myself up off the floor he was sitting up in bed as white as the sheets and yelling, "What's happened?" It frightened me too! A simple case of the unknown and the anticipatory senses being dormant.

If one anticipates something and it does not happen but something else happens instead, then fright can occur very easily and it is this sort of situation that frightens most racing drivers. Obviously the top drivers with wide experience are not easily caught out, but I have talked to many of them who have been frightened when an unexpected incident has occurred. In the case of a crash with another car there is seldom any immediate fright, but afterwards it can occur because, at the time, the conditions were known, but on reflection they realise how close to death they have been and death is the greatest unknown quantity.

A popular misconception has it that racing drivers have "nerves of steel" which is entirely erroneous, for they can all be frightened by some condition or another. What they do have is very wide experience and very active anticipation, which draws on experience and memory to function. We have seen that a driver with good proprioception does not lose his sense of direction or balance during a spin and will drive on afterwards. This is closely connected with fright, for the driver who loses these senses after traversing 90 degrees then gets into the unknown, and when he stops he is in an acute state of fright and a second or two must pass while he readjusts his senses.

As a passenger on sidecars and in 170 m.p.h. sports cars I have never been frightened by any of the actions of the vehicle, for I have always had the "safety valve" of being able to mentally pass all responsibility to one of the world's best riders or drivers. With Eric Oliver we often got into what we called a "dodgy situation" and, while I was always fully conscious of what was happening, I often knew I could not have coped with the situation had I been riding the motor-cycle. The same with Moss; I have been in situations that I knew I could not have dealt with, in all cases because of a lack of ability, but I have known in theory what should be done, so I have mentally relaxed and thought, "It's up to you chum, if you cannot sort this little lot out then no one can." A childlike faith, but not an unreasonable one I feel, for they usually managed to cope. I was not in the unknown and so, in consequence, I was not frightened, and in addition, not being in control of the vehicle, I was not able to appreciate accurately just how close we were to the limit of safety.

On the other hand, when driving myself I have often been frightened by the sudden appearance of an unknown quantity, such a hitting a patch of ice when I have thought the roads where completely free of it. That always sends a cold shiver down my spine for a fraction of a second as the steering goes light, but the instant it happens my senses are made aware of the conditions and fright is replaced by concentration on these new circumstances. In all the spins and crashes I have experienced on two, three and four wheels, I don't think I have ever suffered from fright, because they have all been anticipated—even if only by a tenth of a second. However, I have frightened myself many times when I haven't spun or crashed, for then my anticipatory senses have prepared me for the worst, and when it doesn't arrive I am plunged momentarily into the unknown until I readjust myself, but during that fraction of a second I suffer acute fright. In 1956 in the Mille Miglia I was with Moss in a Maserati and we had a lurid crash that ended up over the edge of a mountain-side with a tree holding the car from plunging three hundred feet down into the valley (20). I am often asked "Weren't you frightened?"; but of course I wasn't, for the whole incident was so straightforward and according to the textbook that at no time was there any unknown factor in our uncontrollable progress. I could see it all coming and anticipate and prepare myself for each eventuality, so there was no cause for fright, only a fascination in seeing what the final outcome was going to be.

The sort of things that really frighten me and make my heart beat faster are those unknown factors that creep up when I am thinking of something else. Any number of times I have been driving quietly along in a completely re-laxed mental state, just conscious of the hum of the engine, when I have passed some road workings and a workman has started up a pneumatic drill. This sudden and violent change of conditions has really frightened me for an instant and I have instinctively reached for the ignition switch thinking my engine had blown up. On one occasion I was riding a motor-cycle along a road that ran parallel to the top of a railway cutting. It was dark, and I was only conscious of the noise of the wind and the beat of the single-cylinder engine. Suddenly an express train came out of a tunnel and into the cutting with such a roar that I swerved violently and nearly fell off. There had been no previous warning of the sudden change of conditions and, not being aware of the presence of the railway lines, I was overcome by "the unknown" for a fraction of a second. My immediate reaction was "Oh crikey, a train" and then all was normal again. Had the engine of my motor-cycle burst underneath me with an equally loud noise I would not have been frightened, for my anticipation was conscious of noise beneath me and any change would not have been entirely unexpected, but the sudden introduction of an unexpected noise on my left was very frightening.

As I have tried to show, the racing driver is not immune to fright, so he is not abnormal, but other parts of his mental make-up encourage him to search for greater experience all the time and this, together with his anticipations, reduces the number of unknown quantities he is likely to be faced with. There are drivers who become frightened, but they do not reach the top and seldom race for very long, and also the top drivers often suffer from a tensed nervous system, especially before a race, but this is an entirely different thing and is really quite a good safety valve. Without this a driver or rider is liable to get into a "speed happy" state, which is a phenomenon that appears occasionally among folk who race. It occurs with racing motor-cyclists more than racing motorists, but the symptoms are the same and, unless curbed, they can prove fatal. It is a state of mind that casts aside caution the moment a certain speed is reached, though more often than not it is possessed by a rider or driver of great skill and he gets away with impossible things for a very long time; either until a bad crash injures him or common sense prevails and he stops racing. I knew two particular motor-cyclists who did a great deal of racing, and both suffered from this "speed happy" sensation. They knew perfectly well what the trouble was, what the outcome would be, and tried hard by will-power to overcome it; but they were both unsuccessful. Wherever they raced they would do well, and both were among the top of the private-owner racers of a few years ago, but they were continually having most spectacular crashes, and by some stroke of fate, always got away lightly. One of them was racing on British circuits, particularly on aerodromes, and in practice would put in some phenomenally fast laps on an ordinary racing machine which compared well with riders of factory machines, but then he would run wide on to the grass, or overdo things in a corner and have the bicycle slide from under him. His mechanic would repeatedly tell him to take things a bit more easily and, though he realised every time he crashed exactly why, he was quite incapable of controlling himself. It was not a question of wild uncontrolled riding, he would simply go faster and faster until the limit was reached, being unable to ease-off as his limit approached.

He would often say that he knew he was "speed happy" and once he got astride a racing motor-cycle all his reason left him, and only his inborn skill kept him alive. On his first visit to the Isle of Man for the T.T. races, over one of the most difficult circuits in the world, he was very aware of the dangers he was running unless he could forcibly slow himself down. At the start of practice he began lapping at an absurdly high speed for someone who had not seen the course before, and at the end of the first practice period he had caused quite a stir by his riding and speed. He knew then that it was foolhardy to go on, but the urge to race was in him and nothing could put him off, and he kept telling himself he had to be strong-willed and overcome this "speed happy" characteristic and be content with reasonably fast lap times. On another practice outing he overdid things and crashed heavily, putting himself in hospital for a time. After that he never rode again, for he realised that to continually ride over the safety limit on small tracks and aerodromes was one thing, but if he was going to be the same on Grand Prix circuits he was not going to live long. It was a great wrench for him to give up, but he had no alternative; he was quite incapable of riding any slower, or not so near the limit.

The other chap was riding in continental races, on road circuits and Grand Prix courses, and he suffered from exactly the same disease of "speed happiness". When he stayed on the bicycle he was phenomenally fast, but he did not stay on it very long. He too was very conscious of his trouble, but also could not do anything about riding any slower. He had a great number of crashes, luckily none of them very serious, but it cost him an awful lot of money in bicycle repairs. Every time he was aware of the cause of the crash—not lack of skill, but not knowing when he was reaching the end of the safety limit. He persevered for a few years, but showed no improvement, though his lap speeds were always good, and rather than tempt fate too far, he also retired while he still had the chance.

The point about these two riders, and there are many more like them, is that they had the ability to become really great riders, if only they could have tempered their dash and speed with a little reason. Off their bicycles they were level-headed young men, knowing all the theory of what constitutes a good rider, but once astride a racing motor-cycle their reason left them.

There have also been car drivers suffering from the same disease, but fewer car drivers race for the sheer love of racing mechanical things, and one accident or frightening moment can often put them off racing before they have really started. The great Argentinian driver Froilan Gonzalez was probably as good an example as any of a "speed happy" driver, and in car racing such men are often described as "lead foot drivers", meaning that they know only one place for their right foot and that is hard on the accelerator— regardless of the consequences. If they have a degree of inborn skill they proceed in a series of wild-looking swerves, having a tendency to use all the road and a lot of the grass verge as well, while if they do not have any inherent skill they spin off on the first bend. Other drivers that come to mind who had a slight touch of the "speed happy" characteristic are Duncan Hamilton, George Abecassis and the late Raymond Sommer. It is a characteristic which is desirable as long as it can be controlled, for it means that the driver will go really fast at all times, which is most praiseworthy, and such a driver is often described as a "press-on type". In a

111

car, you can drive in such a manner and get away with a
great deal, thanks to the inherent stability of the racing car,
and its ability to slide or spin without hurt, but on a motor-
cycle such a characteristic spells disaster, for the margin of
safety when cornering or braking a racing motor-cycle is
very, very small.

Now the interesting thing is just why these people are
affected in the way they are. As the whole process is a
mental one it undoubtedly has some psychological root, but
as yet no investigation has been carried out on such a
driver. It is a pity in some ways that motor racing is not a
state-subsidised science, for then we could hand over one of
the "specimen" drivers to the laboratories and find out the
reasons why he is "speed happy". It has been suggested
that, if it is a simple state of mind, this type of personality
may react to the stimulus of speed, either through the
medium of the eyes, or through the body feeling wind-
pressure on it, and that being thus stimulated it becomes
satisfied, and produces a relaxed mental condition. I think
there is no doubt at all that the actual physical effects of
high speed are satisfying to me—which is why I enjoy high
speeds. It is possible that the "speed happy" characters
are over-stimulated by speed to the point of over-satisfaction,
so that their self-preservation instincts become dulled,
allowing them to go beyond the normal "safety valve" of
the apparent limit, so that they find themselves on the
threshold of the ultimate limit from which only a genius can
return. The world's greatest drivers can deliberately
transgress the apparent limit on a corner and, because the
action is deliberate and calculated, they can return from it,
as their self-preservation instinct, which after all is the
strongest and most powerful of the human instincts, tempers
their action with a degree of caution. The "speed happy"
ones are over-satisfied by reason of the speed, and the
subsequent dulling of the self-preservation instinct allows
them to go into the danger area of the limits of cornering
so that they enter this phase without being wholly aware of
it, and sometimes they can retreat, if the satisfaction is

reduced at this point, but at other times they cannot retreat and then they crash.

This is all closely connected with the psychological reasons that prompt people to race at all. We know that many people masquerade as racing drivers, for being a racing driver these days carries a certain amount of glamour and publicity which appeals to the vanity of some humans. The true racing driver does so for one basic reason, which is that racing or competition satisfies him in a way that everyday life cannot. The human being has a basic quality that makes it a fighter, for not so long ago mere existence against the rigours of nature meant a fight and a struggle, so that Man developed with those qualities in him. As civilization made the act of staying alive an easier and more simple matter Man no longer had the need to fight and struggle, but certain specimens of the genus Man retained these qualities, so they had to look around for outlets. As the natural ones were removed by his own cleverness he had to devise new ones, and motor racing was surely one of them. For this reason people who race, either with cars or motor-cycles, are not average people by any manner of means, and even the most mediocre club racer is surely a cut above the timid human being, conditioned by placid and comfortable surroundings into a state of doing nothing more violent than watching others expend energy.

There is no doubt at all that the more violent the activity chosen by a human being the more unusual will be his character, and motor racing has certainly produced some very colourful characters who, even if not good racing drivers, at least brighten what might be a dull game.

By the present-day standard of what is normal the racing driver is essentially a "freak", and rather a belligerent one at that, who has a part of his brain which would seem to refuse to accept the normal. On numerous occasions I have watched somebody racing, not always good drivers either, and thought, "What is it that makes that chap take up motor racing", and I have invariably come to the conclusion that it is some strange mental need that is being satisfied by the effects of speed, the noise and the knowledge that he is treading on dangerous ground. There is no doubt that certain people obtain immense mental satisfaction from the knowledge that what they are doing is dangerous; it is a psychological reaction to being surrounded by apparent safety, and this could account for the increased activity in racing since the recent war. The stimulus of dangerous living in the time of war probably left its effect on a certain type of human, so that it was dissatisfied at the sudden removal of all danger and looked for an easy way to replace it, either wholly or in part, and the motor-car was a simple and obvious medium to use.

Of course, there are drivers who would appear to race purely for financial reasons—and some of them even admit this—but they are not telling the truth; probably because they are incapable of self-analysis and reasoning. They all do it for a fundamental psychological reason which is stronger in some than in others, and that is why some people are content to be helper to a driver while others only attempt minor racing activities and have no interest in progressing beyond the simple rally or driving test.

CHAPTER IX

ANALYSIS

LET us agree that the racing driver is a freak of the twentieth century, having nothing in common with any freaks of the past, due to the simple fact that the automobile did not appear until the end of the nineteenth century. Let us look a little deeper into his actions.

We hear a lot of vague statements about why one driver is better than another; why some can excel at one and others at another branch of motor racing. Such remarks are "driving with the seat of his pants", or "it's his quick reactions, you know", but the one that probably gets nearer to the truth than any is the remark that a driver is a "natural". This at least admits to driving prowess having some connection with the basic physical and mental faculties with which we are born.

In the term Racing Driver, I want to emphasise once again that I am thinking of the top few, those who reach the greatest heights in the business of racing motor-cars. In other words, the perfectionists, or the drivers who excel at this modern art form, the really high-speed driver, not the fast driver like our friends, and certainly not Mr. Everyman the average driver.

Let us take a very simple situation and analyse it to see exactly what a driver does, and then apply it to the racing driver. If you are driving along a straight road at, let us say, 50 m.p.h. and a dog runs across the road some way in front of you, a chain-reaction starts up which, if nicely controlled and balanced, results in the car stopping before it hits the dog. When the dog appears, the eyes register first, and they inform the brain that an obstruction lies ahead, which the brain interprets into the need for taking precautions. The necessary muscles are energised and the right foot is lifted from the accelerator and placed on the brake pedal. So far we have made use of eyes to collect the new information, the nerves and brain to transmit and understand it, and muscles to respond to it. This process of reaction may be very rapid (indeed the foot may have moved even before we are consciously aware of the dog), but it still takes a certain measurable time, usually termed the reaction time, for completion. Now comes into play judgment; a conscious product of experience and memory in the brain, which modifies the unconscious reflex chain by telling you how hard to apply the brakes in order to stop before striking the dog. Now if, just before the dog appeared from the hedge, a cat crossed the road, going at full speed, but far enough ahead to not be a danger to our car, we could do one of two things. Go through our chain-reaction, unnecessarily we should find, in order to avoid the cat, or we could bring into play our powers of anticipation, which are a product of experience, vision and the association of ideas. On seeing the cat crossing the road flat-out, we should anticipate the appearance of a dog in hot pursuit. Having anticipated that, though not yet seeing it, our reaction chain is prepared, and when the dog appeared our reaction time would be that much less and the response better coordinated.

So now we have five separate parts to our actions—Vision, Nervous Processes, Anticipation, Judgment and Response. If we should happen to be in a very silent car and we heard the approaching bark of a dog, we could substitute Aural for Vision, or if the dog was changed for a smelly cow, we could substitute Smell for Aural. So we see that the first part of our chain is flexible, varying according to which of our natural senses is stimulated; the rest remain the same for any situation. Obviously, as far as extraneous objects that might affect the car are concerned, our racing driver relies on visual senses in his "chain".

Returning to our hypothetical cat and dog "dice"; if we happened to be looking through a pair of binoculars we could see the cat from much further away, and in consequence our chain-reaction could be energised much earlier, which would call for far less braking effort; or alternatively, we could use the same braking power but be travelling at a much greater speed, assuming our braking efficiency to be the same. So if our eyesight is above the average, though not as powerful as binoculars, we could approach the cat-and-dog situation at a much higher speed and, all other things being equal, stop at the same point as someone with weaker eyesight. Just how important eyesight is in high-speed driving I will deal with at greater length later on, but suffice to say that for high-speed driving vision is the all-important sense on which we must rely. As I have shown, the cat preceding the dog, who after all is the real danger, allows our anticipation to assist us. Without anticipation we would have to rely purely on the stimulus of vision.

As an example of how anticipation can help the racing driver I would quote the 1950 Monte Carlo Grand Prix, when Farina, who was lying second on the opening lap, spun at the Harbour Corner and the rest of the field telescoped into him or came to rest. In the lead was Fangio, oblivious of what had happened behind him, and when he arrived on the next lap, only just over a minute and a half after the crash had happened, there was no warning of what lay round the bend, other than a high degree of excitement among the spectators before the corner—especially those who were too far before the corner to see what was going on. The flag marshals were in a high old flap and had abandoned their posts, so there was no official warning of the blocked road, but the agitation of the spectators made itself felt to Fangio as he approached and his anticipatory senses went through an interesting process. The first stimulus, by vision, was that something unusual had happened; as there was nothing unusual in sight on the approach to the corner he recalled that the evening before, while in the Automobile Club, he had been looking at some photographs of a multiple crash in the 1936 Monte Carlo race, and this combination of experience and association of ideas prompted him to slow much earlier than he would have done under normal circumstances and, by the time he arrived at a point where he could see round the corner, he was able to stop.

I experienced a very similar situation in a Mille Miglia race with George Abecassis when we were in the H.W.M.-Jaguar. The crowds who line the road in that race all wave frantically as you pass, mostly with handkerchiefs and newspapers, so that you are conscious of a continuous waving and flapping all along the route in the populated parts. At first you think this fluttering of white means agitation over an accident that lies ahead, but after a while you become used to it, as a background of excitement and enthusiasm. Approaching one small town the usual fluttering could be seen on both sides of the road, but then as we turned a sharp right-hand bend and headed for an equally sharp left-hand bend I was conscious that the hand-waving and fluttering had changed its tempo and there was a distinct air of agitation about it, and when a spectator ran across the road in front of us waving a chair it was obvious that something was up. All this was having the same effect on Abecassis and he slowed right down. Sure enough, as we entered the left-hand bend there was Farina's Ferrari well and truly smashed against the trees. It was still smoking and the road was covered with dirt, gravel and excited crowds, for he had started only a few minutes ahead of us. Although in this instance there was little or no danger to us, the speed at this part of the course being very low so that we could avoid the wreckage easily, it was a perfect example of the stimulus of vision, coupled with anticipation, taking effect before any direct evidence of trouble was available.

If we are agreed on the factors which cause a driver to do something, namely Vision, Nervous Processes, Anticipation, Judgment and Response, let us look at them more closely. The three basic parts of the overall reaction are (1) the sensory system, which is made up of the eyes and nerves to (2) the central nervous system. This is where we have our anticipation and judgment, and the "feedback" from the anticipation returns to our central nervous system; while judgment is coupled to (3) the effector system. This final basic part is made up of the nerves from the central nervous system and the muscles. Any reaction must go through these three basic parts in the pattern described. Our chain reaction might therefore be written as (1) sensory system; (2) central nervous system/anticipation/judgment; (3) response.

Anticipation does not fit well into any one place in the original scheme of five parts, for though it must originate in the brain, it often appears to act even before a visual stimulus has been received, i.e. when everything in view is apparently quite normal. As previously explained it can in this way assist deficient vision by ensuring that the reaction chain is primed, and the time lost by slow visual recognition of danger is made up by faster response. In a similar way other parts of the chain are interrelated, and the effect of the poor performance of a weak one may be ameliorated by the others. This applies less to vision and judgment than to the others, and if we are weak in these our overall efficiency is impaired irreparably.

It is a fairly simple thing to analyse oneself in this connection, and it is extremely interesting. I have found that I possess very good anticipation, below standard vision, excellent nervous processes, good response and mediocre judgment, which all adds up to a very limited ability as a high-speed driver. Naturally one cannot arrive at one's own analysis easily and quickly, for it requires a number of experimental examples to permit a valuation to be placed on certain of them. Examples of anticipation are easy to come by providing you have done a good deal of driving, preferably fairly fast, while vision can be checked with optical instruments. Reaction times can be measured on a machine, and indicate the efficiency of the nervous processes, though this method is not infallible, as some people have short reaction times at low speeds, and no shorter at high speeds, while others improve with speed, but at least the machine can indicate a trend. Reaction times are a question of honest self-analysis, deciding after an incident, however trivial and

119

not necessarily connected with a motor-car, whether you reacted as quickly as you could have done. Such vague remarks as "sharp-witted" or "keeps his wits about him" float about the edges of this analysis. Finally judgment is a straightforward measurement against a datum; by comparison with a cross-section of friends it is easy to see how one's judgment stands up.

If we give our five factors a percentage efficiency, then the perfect driver will have 100% on each count, but so far it is not possible to decide on a maximum efficiency; we can only take the known best as 100%, and as time passes we find new standards against which to make measurements. In present-day racing Fangio and Moss are two of the accepted standards, and they both have all five parts of their "chain" in a very high state of efficiency. The visual ability and time of nervous transmission to and from the brain are fixed, these being fundamental parts of the human physical make-up which cannot be altered under normal circumstances. I know they can be affected by various stimulants, but here I am considering a natural static condition. The nervous processes within the brain take a certain time and this may be shortened a little by experience. Anticipation is closely bound up with experience and intelligence and can definitely be improved upon, as can judgment, while the muscular responses can be improved in accuracy and coordination.

Taking our two standards of efficiency, Fangio and Moss, there is little to choose between them under normal conditions, though it is possible that Fangio's anticipation is slightly superior to that of Moss, while their judgment shows little variation. On the other hand, some drivers show less anticipation, but make up for this deficiency with apparently remarkable reaction times. It is interesting that the things that let down a perfectionist are anticipation and judgment. When a first-class driver has an accident it is usually as a result of false anticipation, or a lack of it at the precise moment required, or the result of a false piece of judgment. Recently Fangio ran off the road in a sports Maserati in

Buenos Aires due to experimenting and trying to take a corner in third gear instead of second as he had been doing (21). His judgment of the maximum possible speed for the corner was in error and he went off the road. In Venezuela in 1957 Moss hit another competitor because he did not, in fact could not, anticipate that the other car was going to turn across his path.

In these two examples the perfectionists showed that the mere human being is not infallible and his two weaknesses are anticipation and judgment. Now both these factors depend largely upon experience, so we can say that our top drivers require the physical properties of good vision, an excellent nervous system and well-trained muscular responses, and then experience will build up their anticipation and judgment. By experience I do not mean merely racing experience, but overall experience of causes and effects as applied to the human being and which control his whole life beyond the two natural instincts of self-preservation and procreation. Almost every other factor that has a bearing on life is a product of environment, and from that experience is gained and judgment developed to deal with conditions under which the individual is placed. In our case, the Racing Driver, the environment is motor racing and the conditions those of danger and hardship, so the natural "learning ability" gains experience and develops judgment to deal with these conditions. The human being or Racing Driver is in effect a servo-mechanism into which is fed information, and the output is the maintaining of stability for given conditions, in our case motor racing and race winning. As with all servo-mechanisms there is a certain amount of "feed-back" from the output end which is put back into the mechanism again, and with the Racing Driver this takes the form of experience. It would be a simple matter to build a servo-mechanism to deal with a racing car, the object of which would be race-winning, but it would have two failings, which so far cannot be reproduced very easily mechanically. These are the human attributes of anticipation and judgment. But as we have seen they are the two factors which are most likely to cause the Racing Driver to fail as a 100% efficient machine, so we can now ponder on the possibilities of replacing our driver with a servo-mechanism, or a number of such mechanisms, and under conditions of "failure" our mechanism would probably be an improvement, for we could reproduce vision, the nervous processes and response to higher degrees of accuracy than the human ones. If we accept that a weakness in any of the links in our chain could be counteracted to a small degree by the other links, then a superlative mechanism to reproduce vision might make up for "no anticipation", and a mechanism giving instantaneous response to a decision of the "black box" could assist "no judgment". At the moment the great drivers such as Fangio, Moss, Hawthorn, Behra, Brooks and company have such high degrees of anticipation and judgment, developed by experience and learning ability, that any weakness in the other factors they might have does not lower the overall picture sufficiently to put them in any danger of being superseded by a collection of servo-mechanisms and mechanical brains. However, it is pretty certain that the knowledge is available to produce a "mechanical driver" that could improve on some racing drivers for given conditions. And just as some drivers would be certain to have accidents, so too would our "mechanism", but I would go so far as to predict that the "mechanical driver" would not have such a "clue-less" accident as some drivers I have seen!

Already mechanisms are capable of "learning" from experience and it is possible to construct a mechanism to have a memory, so perhaps the day is not far off when we can install anticipation and judgment into a mechanism of a sufficiently high degree of efficiency to deal with all the conditions prevailing in motor racing. If that is so, then the days of the human being as a Racing Driver are numbered, just as the days of the pilot are rapidly coming to an end. That would be so, of course, if motor racing were a science and not a sport and if it were supported by governments and not by philanthropists. As the scene is at present the chance of the motor-racing organisers accepting an entry of a Grand Prix car driven by a "black box" is remote. But the thought of a box that ticks and buzzes and sends and receives information which is computed by the team manager in the pits, surrounded by an entourage of "boffins" in white coats controlling knobs and switches and reading dials, is indeed an intriguing one for those of us who have a "scientific" outlook on racing.

As our Racing Driver at present is strictly "human" let us continue with our analysis of him and consider the all-important factor of vision. There is no doubt that eyesight plays a very important part in the physical make-up of a racing driver, and it is usual to find that the best drivers have exceptional eyesight which is well above average. At one time I had a photostat copy of an article I had written, taken from the page in the original magazine, the only difference being that my copy was only about one inch high, as against the twelve inches of the journal from which it was taken. Even though I knew the article well I could not read the small type without the aid of a magnifying glass; the purpose of this reproduction was merely to provide an example of how the machine that produced it would diminish without losing clarity, and I showed it to Stirling Moss as a joke, suggesting that it was a new economy size for our magazine. Imagine my amazement when he took it from me and read it out loud without the slightest hesitation. I was so incredulous that I suggested he must know the opening lines of the article from memory, having seen the original, but to convince me he read, just as easily, a paragraph halfway down the page. I tried as hard as I could, even with my supposedly corrective spectacles, but I was quite unable to read a word.

This casual incident started a train of thought and later I showed this diminutive print to some other first-class racing drivers and they all read it without the slightest hesitation. I began to think that my eyes and spectacles were in a bad way, until I showed it to a friend who does not motor race, and he had as much difficulty as I did. Trying this test on a number of people I was able to find some who could not read it, like myself, others who read a word here or there, or faltered through a few lines and then gave up as the strain was too great, and some who read it as easily as the racing drivers, but were not drivers themselves. This proof of the great difference in eyesight at short distances between what is accepted as average, and exceptional sight, was most revealing and much wider than I would ever have expected.

While being driven fast by capable drivers I have often had examples of how they could see things much further ahead than I, and two of the most outstanding examples were again given by Stirling Moss during our drives in the Mille Miglia. During the 1955 race we were travelling at about 150–160 m.p.h. along a straight when Moss suddenly pointed over his shoulder and looking back I could just see a car in the distance. It was the late Eugenio Castellotti, in his 4·4-litre Ferrari, who was gaining on our Mercedes-Benz. At first I thought Moss had pointed to suggest that I should look to see if anyone was catching us, but on reflection I realised that the gesticulation was too definite; he obviously knew someone was behind, and then I realised that the only way he could have known was by seeing the car in the rear-view mirror. Now looking into a rear-view mirror at 60 m.p.h. is one thing, but to look into one at 160 m.p.h. is a very different proposition, and at that speed to be able to spot a car in the distance showed remarkable control of his vision. At the speeds we were travelling the sight has to be trained a very long way ahead, so far in fact that I am certain my personal vision for distances is inadequate to drive at 150 m.p.h. on the open road. To be able to focus half a mile ahead, change the focus to a mirror eighteen inches from the eyes, look into the mirror half a mile behind, and return to the original forward vision, obviously requires excellent lenses and eye-muscles.

During another Mille Miglia we were travelling down the long stretches of road leading into Pescara on the Adriatic coast, and Moss pointed ahead with a signal we had previously arranged to mean another competitor. I looked ahead, but could see nothing remotely resembling another car; as far as I was concerned the road ahead was quite clear for perhaps a mile or more. This occasion again took place at over 160 m.p.h., and as the road bent slightly or went over a brow it was obvious that Moss was losing sight of his quarry, for every now and then it would reappear to him and he would give me another encouraging signal. I just nodded, or gave him a thumbs-up sign, but I still could not see any car ahead of us. It must have been some minutes before I saw a tiny speck way ahead in the distance, but whether it was a car or a dog in the road I could not tell, and merely assumed it was the car which Moss had seen so much earlier. A few minutes later we were close enough for me to see that it was a red car, and by the low tail it was pretty certainly a 3-litre Maserati, but I knew not who. I looked at my list of runners to check on who it might be, but I need not have bothered for Moss could already see and recognise the driver's helmet and he again signalled to me, with our code sign for Perdisa, and sure enough some time later I could see for myself that it was Cesare Perdisa.

Now, while the two instances I have given show that the measurably superior vision of a top racing driver enables him to keep a check on the progress of the race, relative to himself, it has a much more important use. As we have already discussed, one of the most important faculties in a top driver is the factor of anticipation and its connection to the reflexes. The driver who can see two hundred yards further than the next man has a very great advantage, for it means that he gets an earlier view of an obvious change of conditions, or an earlier indication of a possible change of conditions. Again, as I have already mentioned, a driver can make up for a slight deficiency in one of the faculties by a super-efficiency in another, so that a driver with exceptional eyesight and normal anticipation could obtain the same results as a driver with normal eyesight but above-normal anticipation. When you get a driver with both faculties above normal then you have an exceptional one, assuming of course that his other faculties are in order.

Taking this question of vision to the minimum and to an absurd degree, if you consider driving in fog on an unknown road, so that the limiting factor is forward vision, then the man with good eyesight will be able to travel faster than the man with bad eyesight, all other conditions being equal. As your eyesight became worse, so would you drive slower, and conversely the better your eyesight the faster you are able to drive, excluding for the moment all the other factors.

In an article he wrote, Paul Frère gave a good example of the importance of eyesight during his testing with Jaguar, when he had the wrong goggles on. While he thought he could see adequately, he did not realise how handicapped he was until he tried again with another pair of goggles and then went a lot faster without any obvious conscious effort.

The fact that first-rate vision is essential for a top driver is rather indicated by the fact that very few really good high-speed drivers wear spectacles. About the only exceptions to this rule were B. Bira and Bob Gerard, the former wearing lensed goggles and the latter spectacles and a visor, but even so neither of them was in the top rank of Grand Prix drivers, while today Masten Gregory wears spectacles but I would predict that vision will prevent him ever being World Champion. Villoresi wore spectacles while in the front rank of Grand Prix drivers, but in his youth his vision was normal and he gained top-line racing experience which compensated for the later poor vision.

Anyone who has been fortunate enough to talk to Fangio, or to be close enough to him to observe his eyes, cannot have helped noticing their remarkable sharpness. There is no doubt that eyesight plays a very vital part in Fangio's success, which is quite remarkable for a man in his late forties. There are times when he appears to be taking no interest in his surroundings and appears to be in a sleepy and lethargic mood, but watch his eyes closely and you will see that they are observing everything going on around him. Though he moves his head very slowly, mostly due to the neck injury he received in a crash at Monza in 1952, and in normal everyday life his whole body moves slowly, his eyes will flash from one thing to another with great rapidity, which is made all the more noticeable by these slow body movements. It is interesting to read in his biography[1] these words about Fangio as a young man in 1939, after one of the gruelling long-distance races in South America: ". . . a young man came in. His eyes were clear in spite of the immense tiredness which showed on his rather chubby face, his hair was brown in colour, and as he walked quietly into the room he said, in a flat tone, *'Buen provecho'*."

Those eyes are still clear and they are the eyes of a remarkable man; a man with terrific ability with a racing car, and with a personal charm and character which caused legends to be created about him while he was still at the height of his career. A most worthy World Champion. If you have not been lucky enough to stand close to the great man, study some photographs of him and note the remarkable brightness and clearness of his eyes, even when his face looks tired and weary after a gruelling race.

We have seen how vision plays a very important part in the physical make-up of a good driver, and Fangio is indeed an excellent corroboration of this fact.

[1] *The Life Story of Juan Manuel Fangio,* by R. Hansen and F. B. Kirbus (Pearl, Cooper Ltd.)

CHAPTER X

THEORY

A GREAT deal of information is available today about the handling characteristics of motor-cars, both passenger vehicles and racing cars, and it is the latter with which we are particularly concerned. In fairly simple and straightforward terms, what a car does and why can be described in technical language, and of particular interest to us is the fact that this data can be illustrated by means of a simple graph. Because there is now sufficient knowledge to make this possible, the technical relationship between the racing car designer and the racing driver could be a lot closer, providing the driver was in possession of a reasonable comprehension of the relevant facts. We shall consider the handling characteristics of racing cars and they will be illustrated by a number of curves, and I shall then co-relate the curves with drivers to show how a driver with an intimate knowledge of the science of roadholding and cornering could improve his driving. What is more important is that we shall also see how some drivers can achieve situations and results without this knowledge, by an inborn sensitivity which will be discussed later.

First of all we have to agree, or rather accept, a number of basic principles, and one of these is that when a tyre is deflected from the straight-running path it assumes an angle to the direction of travel, due to deformation of the tread pattern and the structural characteristics of the pneumatic tyre. This angle is known as the "slip-angle", and everyone, from Auntie in her "Anglia" to Fangio in his Maserati, generates slip-angles at the contact area of the tyres with the road. In the case of Auntie these are very small angles;

in the case of Fangio they are very big.   In Fig. 22 we see
the plot of side-thrust against slip-angle for a typical rubber
tyre.   This was obtained by turning the tyre from a slip-
angle of 30° to the left to a slip-angle of 30° to the right, and
measuring the side-thrust resisted by the tyre.   As it is
obvious that the maximum cornering ability of a car is when

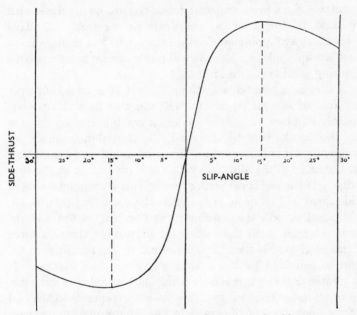

22   Side-thrust and slip-angle for a typical rubber tyre

the four tyres generate the maximum amount of side-thrust,
it will be appreciated that the curve in Fig. 22, which is for
an individual tyre, shows to the right and left of the vertical
centre line increasing cornering power for the tyre up to a
slip-angle around 15°, after which the capacity to withstand
side-thrust diminishes gradually.   There is a popular misconception that tyre adhesion breaks down completely after
a slip-angle of 15° but this is not so, as is shown in the
diagram; it merely reaches a peak around this point and
then diminishes.   The actual maximum slip-angle is not

129

constant and varies for different tyres and conditions, but for our hypothetical considerations we can take 15° as the maximum slip-angle which is desirable. The point at which the cornering power of the tyre begins to deteriorate is known as the "break-away" point. When this point is passed it does not mean that the car will slide helplessly out of control, but it does mean that control will not be so readily available, for a high cornering force, C_f, will be involved with reduced frictional properties available to resist it. This "break-away" point is of vital interest to the racing driver just as slip-angles are, and it will not go amiss to discuss this limiting condition more fully.

A tyre is in contact with the road, not at a point, but over an area of several square inches, and this area is approximately elliptical in shape. When a small cornering force is applied to the tyre by the road, the contribution made by different parts of the contact area varies uniformly from zero at the front of the elliptical patch to a maximum at the rear edge. If the car is cornering gently, this maximum value of side force will be quite low, but as the cornering thrusts are increased so will the maximum at the rear of the contact area increase, until there comes a time when the side force demanded at this part becomes equal to the maximum that can be provided by the available coefficient of friction. If a greater demand is made then this part of the tyre will slide in relation to the road, and this stage corresponds to the end of the linear part of the graph in Fig. 22 and in a typical case would represent a slip-angle of about 5°.

As the degree of cornering increases, this sliding part of the contact area will gradually extend forward over the whole ellipse, until finally there is complete sliding relative to the road. When the whole contact area has reached a state of sliding the condition is called break-away, and this is reached at the break-away point, represented in Fig. 22 by the peak of the curve at about 15°. The side-thrust being generated at this point will naturally vary with the size of the tyre and its design as well as with the load being carried. For example, a racing car with special large-section tyres

130

carrying a relatively small load could reach a maximum side-thrust at only 10° slip-angle, and the maximum thrust could be much higher than that generated by a production tyre carrying the weight of a fully-laden saloon, even though the latter was at a slip angle of 15°. The larger the tyre section for the same load, the smaller the slip-angle for the same cornering force, or, conversely, for a maximum C_f and a constant load a bigger-section tyre would generate a small slip-angle.

Looking back on the matter of slip-angle relative to tyre section and load, we can now see that this is the explanation for the fact that fitting oversize tyres on the rear wheels of an inherently oversteering car, such as a pre-war Austin Seven, Frazer Nash, early Porsche or VW, will reduce the amount of oversteer; in other words we shall have made the rear slip-angles approximate more to the front slip-angles, and with some cars such a change of rear tyre section will promote understeer.

For practical purposes we will assume 15° to be the desirable maximum and Auntie probably never generates more than 2° or 3° at the most, whereas Fangio and the "boys" spend most of their racing life in the 10° to 14° bracket. It is the ability to drive a car at these high slip-angles in which we are going to become interested. Now, due to various factors built into the design of cars, the front tyres do not necessarily adopt the same slip-angles as the rear tyres for a given condition of cornering, and there are a multitude of ways in which these front and rear slip-angles can be altered, fundamentally or at will, whilst in motion; however, these factors do not concern us at the moment, suffice to accept that front and rear tyres have independent slip-angles. If they happen to be exactly the same, then the condition is known as neutral steer; if the front slip-angles are greater than the rear then the car is in a condition of understeer, and if the rear slip-angles are greater then the car is in a condition of oversteer. This is a very simple and basic evaluation of the three conditions of cornering under which a motor-car may exist. It is nowadays a simple matter to design a car to operate, on a given corner at a given speed, in any of the three states, and while constant oversteer causes a car to be unstable, constant understeer is a more practical state of affairs, but a mixture of the two is considered by many designers to be the ideal for a racing car. Exactly why this should be so will make itself clear as we progress. A state of continual neutral steer is also possible to achieve, but is not desirable.

As the aim of the racing driver is to get round corners as quickly as possible, it will be appreciated that the overall value of C_f is the important factor, and as this is the sum of the cornering force on all four tyres it is self-evident that if either end of the car can only generate a small C_f value then the overall C_f will consequently be small; on the other hand, if both ends generate the maximum C_f then the total for the car will be the maximum possible, and this would be a state of neutral steer; due to human limitations in receiving information in the brain at high values of C_f and then translating them into mechanical properties, this is not desirable. Also, we shall see how the specialised human being, or racing driver, can achieve better results by having a flexible C_f value at one end or other of a racing car, so that various instincts and reflexes can attain a high total C_f value with greater safety than by an inbuilt high C_f due to neutral steer, when the conditions are approaching "break-away".

The clever racing-car designer will endeavour to achieve a good balance between the characteristics of the two ends of the car and adjust these to the known characteristics of his driver, but we are getting a little ahead of ourselves. To make these steering conditions more easy to consider it is a simple matter to trace them out on a curve and in Fig. 23 is shown the basic "handling characteristic curve layout". The line O—C_f represents, from left to right, a value we will call Cornering Force, which is related to the speed of the car and the radius of the corner, or in other words, the centrifugal force. The left-hand end of the line relates to the car when it is stationary or travelling in a straight line, or when the cornering force is zero. As the car corners C_f increases and we move to the right along O—C_f.

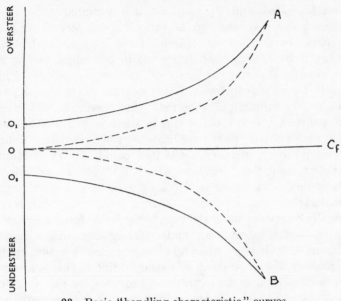

23   Basic "handling characteristic" curves

As we have seen, oversteer is the condition when the rear slip-angles are greater than the front slip-angles and understeer is vice versa.   In Fig. 23 we let the vertical component represent the difference in degrees of the front and rear total slip-angles.   Taking the front slip-angle value from the rear value will leave us with a positive value for oversteer, represented by the vertical component above the line $O—C_f$ and the negative component or understeer by the vertical component below $O—C_f$.   Therefore the area above this line represents the condition of oversteer, and the area below the condition of understeer, for various values of cornering force C_f.   Now it should be obvious that the line $O—C_f$ also represents the condition of neutral steer, being the condition between the other two factors, and the fact that it is represented by a line and not an area will make it obvious that the condition of neutral steer is a very fine one.

The broken line $O—A$ represents the characteristic of a car with oversteer that increases continually as the cornering

133

force increases, and O_1—A illustrates a similar car. The difference between the two indicates that the second car has oversteer even when no cornering force is applied, which is to say it oversteers when travelling in a straight line or is practically stationary. This, of course, is absurd and purely hypothetical, but it illustrates the point that a car can have a handling characteristic that need not start from the point O. Such a car would be inherently unstable and such cars existed; they were unstable when travelling along a straight road, in other words they could not travel in an exact straight line. Anyone who has driven a very early "Chummy" Austin Seven will appreciate this condition. Similarly the broken line O—B represents a car with continually increasing understeer as the cornering force increases, and O_2—B illustrates an understeering car with a basic amount of understeer when no cornering force is acting upon it, namely when travelling in a straight line. This is a very stable condition and for practical purposes we can assume that any car which will travel in a straight line without the necessity to make corrections on the steering has a basic understeer. Going back to our original precepts, the front tyres are generating greater slip-angles than the rear, and further study of this situation by an analysis of the forces involved would show that this is an inherently stable condition, but for our purposes we will accept this as read.

A car with constant understeer is a very practical proposition. American cars have this characteristic, as do many European passenger cars, while racing cars have also been designed to this layout, but practice has shown that it is not ideal when dealing with high values of C_f. It will be readily seen from Fig. 23 that, if the value of understeer is being measured in relation to a factor involving slip-angles, then when the C_f is very high, or we are considering a point far to the right of our datum line, then the maximum slip-angle is approached more and more rapidly and the point at which break-away is reached is arrived at with increasing rapidity. We shall deal later with what can be done when this point is reached and we shall see that in a continual understeer corrections are nigh on impossible, whereas in a state of continual oversteer, or at the end of the line $O—A$, it is possible to effect corrections. For normal passenger car travel a constant understeer is quite practical, for few people reach the higher values of C_f under normal road driving conditions, but for racing Fangio and the "boys" require to drive amongst the high C_f values all the time, so that oversteer in this part of the graph is desirable. We have already seen that oversteer in the lower C_f values, and

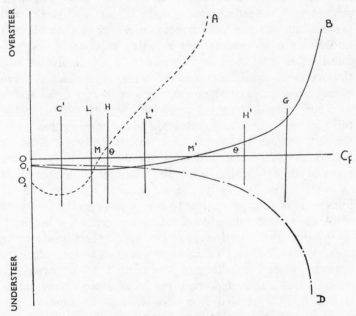

24 Handling characteristic curves for a typical family saloon and two racing cars

especially when C_f is zero, is to be avoided, so what we need to achieve is a combination of the two conditions.

Fig. 24 shows on the dotted line $O_2—A$ the characteristics of many of today's family saloons. They begin with a basic amount of understeer, to ensure that they run in a straight line when no cornering force is applied, and this understeer increases as C_f increases to begin with. The average driver of the family car can be assumed to operate in the range of cornering forces covered by $O—C^1$, in other words the average driver does not corner very fast on the normal road, and by designing the car with understeer it makes it fundamentally very stable for the conditions required by the consumer. However, if the car is fully laden, and has the trunk filled to capacity and perhaps a roof-rack as well, and the driver increases C_f, then due to a number of factors connected with weight-transfer, rear-axle geometry, tyre-loading etc. a state of less understeer will prevail, and on some well-known family cars this condition of understeer deteriorates very rapidly, approaching a condition of neutral steer and passing uncontrollably on into the oversteer conditions as C_f increases. We must all have experienced a heavily-laden family car feeling quite stable on a corner and then suddenly, with very little warning, the tail slides outwards and correction of the steering has to be applied. It can be caused, as I have said, by a number of factors involving the design of the car, but it is neither necessary nor desirable to design a car with a characteristic as in $O_2—A$ in Fig. 24, yet many cars are like this, usually because it is a simple matter to design a car to the first part of the curve, but difficult to obtain this and not the final half. As few owners of family cars go beyond C^1 the manufacturer is safe in overlooking the higher values of C_f and the ultimate outcome of the handling of the car. I have personally damned many manufacturers' products because they act as shown by the dotted line $O_2—A$, due to fundamental deficiencies in the design, but I am invariably told that the car was not meant to be driven at such high cornering powers! I have sympathy for the unfortunate owners of these vehicles who get into the higher C_f values, through no fault of their own, such as when they have to take sudden avoiding action, but that is neither here nor there.

Our racing car has got to operate at higher C_f values, so obviously the dotted line $O_2—A$ will be no use for us, for apart from the change from understeer to oversteer being sudden it also means that this change occurs over a very narrow range of cornering force, shown by the lines L and H on our graph. It can be readily appreciated that the distance between these two lines represents a small increase in cornering force, yet it also represents the difference between a fairly large understeer and a fairly large oversteer, and this means that between cornering forces to the value of L and H, the driver has to make corrections with the controls of the car. Therefore, it becomes obvious that the angle θ made by the handling characteristic line as it crosses the datum line is one that is of vital interest to us. The smaller this angle the more gentle will be the change-over from one condition to the other, and from this it follows that large values of understeer at low C_f values will of necessity mean large θ angles, therefore our racing car does not want too much initial understeer, so that we can keep θ small. The actual point of change-over we will call M, and it will be seen that for a nominal understeer of O_1, the smaller will be θ and the further along our datum line will be M, which will mean that our change from one condition to the other will occur at a much higher cornering force—not speed remember —but cornering force, a value relative to speed and radius of corner. The solid line O_1—B in Fig. 24 shows a suitable curve for a racing car where M^1 is a long way along O—C_f, so that the car goes on understeering until quite high cornering forces are reached, and because of this θ is very small and the L^1 and H^1 values for this car are spread wide apart, allowing the driver a great range of C_f over which to apply corrective forces for the changing conditions. Such a car, when it reached a cornering power of G, would begin to break away on the rear wheels first, and this would build up fairly rapidly, because obviously C_f must have a maximum value and the closer you are to the line O—C_f when this is reached the steeper will be the tail of the curve. Later we shall go on to consider what is happening between the points H^1 and G, and we shall see that for certain corners it is desirable to operate on this part of the curve, sharp corners in particular calling for this characteristic. Returning to the centre part of our curve we can see that the further apart are L^1 and H^1 then the easier our car is to control at one of the most critical points in its handling, and this type of car is usually referred to as a "well-mannered and well balanced" car. I am happy to say that some of our family car manufacturers are beginning to appreciate the desirability of making a study of the point M and the angle θ, and the new Fords and Hillmans in particular are of a very high standard.

For a long fast corner, such as Abbey Curve at Silverstone, or Fordwater at Goodwood, and particularly the Ascari Curve at Monza, it is more desirable to have constant understeer, for it makes the car more stable and easier to drive, and the line O_1—D in Fig. 24 shows the curve of a car that would be good for such corners. It would have a reasonable amount of understeer at very high cornering forces, but would inevitably have to end in final understeer or front-end breakaway, which we shall see later is undesirable. Having kept the car in an understeer condition to such a high value of C_f, if we made it a final oversteerer the crossing of the neutral line would be very steep, i.e. θ would be large and it would be a difficult car to control, for when the change-over took place it would be at such a high cornering force and over such a small range that the mere human being would not be able to cope with it. O_1—D is rather indicative of the Super Squalo Ferrari designed by Aurelio Lampredi in 1953–55, which is the reason why it felt very good on fast circuits such as Monza or Spa but terrible at Monaco and Zandvoort.

By now it should begin to be obvious that the perfect racing car is going to require an infinitely variable number of handling characteristic curves in order to cope with all the circuits and corners involved in motor racing. This would indeed be desirable, but obviously is not yet a practical proposition, so that the designer must decide what his car is going to be used for and then make a compromise amongst all the possible variations. When you start to consider the finer points of this question it can be shown that it is possible by design to make the handling characteristic curve some-what flexible, but what is more interesting to us is that a really clever driver can use certain qualities of a Grand Prix car to change the shape of the handling curve to suit various requirements, and it is this ability which we will now con-sider. However, before we delve too deeply into this matter I must ask the reader to suffer a little more theory, in order to make the final conclusions more readily understandable.

Before leaving this subject it is interesting to note that it is possible to alter the geometry of all four wheels of the single-seater Lotus, independently, in order to achieve the desired "handling characteristic curve" for any given corner. On certain experimental Connaughts this could also be achieved.

CHAPTER XI

UNDERSTEER

WHEN a wheel and tyre are cornering it can easily be proved that, in the absence of any braking or driving torque, that is when revolving freely, the cornering force must act at right-angles to the plane of the wheel. On reaching the break-away point, this cornering force C reaches a limiting value and thereafter stays substantially constant over the range of slip-angles which concerns us in this discussion. This limiting value we will call F, which is equal to $\mu \times W$, where W is the weight supported by the tyre and μ is the coefficient of friction between the road and the tyre. If we now apply a driving or braking torque to the wheel, additional force has to be supplied at the area of contact, which is not possible without increasing the coefficient of friction, our value of W, of course, being unchanged. It follows therefore, that the cornering force C must be reduced until the resultant of the cornering and braking

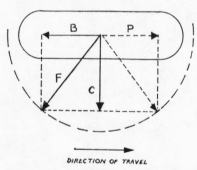

forces does not exceed the maximum attainable value F. This state of affairs is depicted in Fig. 25 where B is a braking force, F the maximum value of $\mu \times W$, and C the resultant cornering force. Alternatively we could replace B with a propulsive force P acting in the opposite direction, in which case F would swing

25 Forces acting on a wheel and tyre when cornering

round towards the direction of travel. In this way F can be made to point in any desired direction as indicated by the broken semicircle, whose radius represents the maximum value of $F = \mu \times W$. If F was pointing straight back the diagram would represent travelling in a straight line with a force B large enough to lock the wheel. When F pointed straight forward it would indicate that an acceleration force P had been applied, so large that the wheel was spinning. By lesser amount of power or braking, the vector F can be rotated to any desired position by a driver who has sufficient skill and sufficient power at his disposal; brakes invariably being capable of locking wheels.

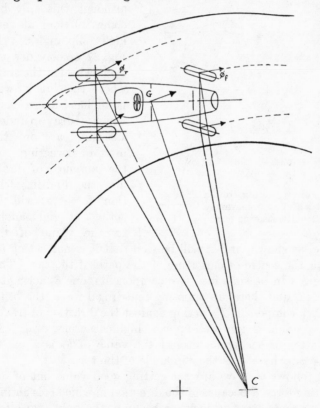

26   Forces acting on the wheels of a car when cornering

In Fig. 26 we see a diagram of a car cornering, the centre of curvature being at the point C, and it will be noticed that, because of the slip-angles developed by the tyres, the car has a pronounced nose-in attitude to the corner, the actual value of this attitude-angle being ϕ_r. These slip-angles (ϕ_f at the front and ϕ_r at the rear) are shown greatly exaggerated for clarity, and ϕ is the angle between the direction in which the tyre is actually travelling and that in which it is pointing, so that all cars corner with the nose

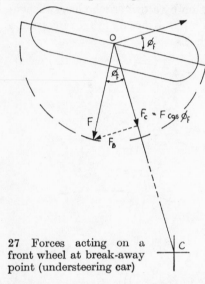

pointing towards the kerb however slowly they may be going, although this only becomes obvious at very high slip-angles. In Fig. 27 we consider one front wheel at the stage where the break-away point has been reached, which is to say an understeering car on the limit of cornering. In the absence of braking, the limiting friction force F will be acting at right-angles to the plane of the

27 Forces acting on a front wheel at break-away point (understeering car)

wheel as shown, and it will be seen that it is not acting towards the centre of curvature of the path of the car. This force F can be split into two components, one F_c acting towards C and therefore opposing centrifugal force, the other smaller component F_B acting against the direction of travel, and producing the well-known high-cornering drag. As a matter of academic interest the value of F_c is equal to $F \cos \phi_f$, where ϕ_f is the slip-angle of the tyre.

It follows that we are not getting good value out of our limiting force F because of the direction in which it is acting. Giving more steering lock, or braking, the only two alternatives we can apply to a front wheel, will swing the vector F rearwards, as shown in Fig. 25, and make the conditions worse, so that the front of the car will run wider, for F_c will become smaller. If we could swing F forwards so that it was pointing directly towards C, then the cornering force would be increased, but this can only be done, *vide* Fig. 25, by applying a propulsive force to the front wheel. This would call for front-wheel-drive and is one reason why cars such as the DS19 Citroën and D.K.W. are stable when cornered under power and less stable on the overrun or with the brakes on.

With a final understeering car, with normal rear-wheel-drive, i.e. one that reaches the break-away point on the front wheels first, there is nothing the driver can do with the steering or front brakes which will increase the cornering force available—generally his efforts will merely make the car run wider still until it runs out of road on the outside of the bend and, because the rear wheels will not have reached the break-away point, it follows that the car as a whole is not attaining the ultimate cornering speed possible. The only hope the driver has of regaining a small amount of control when these final understeer conditions are operative is to remove some of the steering lock, but the point at which to do this is a very fine one and hardly likely to be noticed by the average driver as he goes off the road in an understeer break-away.

Now there is another way out of the trouble and that is to reduce the slip-angles of the rear tyres, for we have seen that in the condition postulated in Fig. 26 the front tyres are on the break-away point while the rear ones are some amount away from their break-away point: in other words the car is in an understeer. We have seen that there is little to be done to help the front tyres by any direct action, but we can help them indirectly and the way to do this is to reduce the cornering force of the rear tyres, and if we can do this sufficiently we can change our understeer to oversteer and in consequence change the direction of the car, which, after all, is our ultimate objective. In Fig. 25 we have seen that

143

a large braking force or a large propulsive force will swing F backwards or forwards until C is reduced to zero, so therefore if we can lock the rear wheels or spin them we can reduce the cornering power of our rear tyres to below that of the front tyres, and change our understeering car into an oversteering one, which will automatically change its direction of travel—always providing there is enough road left. Once the F value of the front tyres starts to diminish it does so rapidly, so that we must reduce the F of our rear tyres almost instantaneously so as to catch and pass the diminishing F of the front tyres. It will be appreciated that all this is happening at high cornering forces, so that it seems highly unlikely that mere mortals like you and me will have much hope of achieving this. Our racing driver, because of his more highly-tuned natural faculties, can sometimes achieve this perilous way out of a difficult situation, and one way of doing it is to jam the gearlever into a lower gear and let the clutch in violently, the sudden reversal load causing the rear wheels to lose adhesion momentarily. The application of wheelspin to reduce the F value at the rear is purely theoretical, because it could not be achieved instantaneously and the time taken for the power to build up to wheelspin proportions would be too long. If modern understeering cars were fitted with large old-fashioned hand-brakes, operating on the rear wheels only, the use of such a brake to lock the wheels would have the desired effect.

When learning all about the foregoing theory I tended to be sceptical until, during the 1956 Mille Miglia, I was able to experience an exact instance of the problem just described. As usual Moss was the driver, and the car was an experimental $3\frac{1}{2}$-litre Maserati sports car which had constant understeer. On one particular corner, a right-hander, the front tyres reached break-away point and as they did so, having "felt" the break-away through the torque he was applying to the rim of the steering wheel, Moss instantaneously flicked the gear-lever from fourth into second gear, locked the rear wheels for a moment and this changed the direction of the car and we continued unscathed. Of course, as passenger,

I could not appreciate what was happening until afterwards, for unless you are holding the steering wheel you have no feel of understeer. I was only conscious of the front apparently going at an angle heading for a wall on the outside of the bend, a movement by Moss with his left hand on the gearlever and then the thought that the tail of the car was sliding outwards. At this point I removed my arm from the cockpit side and tucked it down beside me, gave a small thought to the eighteen-gallon fuel tank that was acting as an armrest, and resigned myself to a crash where the side of the car was going to smack into the wall.

The whole operation of the theory we have been studying could not have occupied more than 4/5ths of a second but it was just sufficient, and while the car changed direction and stopped sliding we reached the end of the corner and were able to continue on up the road. It was one of those incidents after which Moss blows through pursed lips and shakes the tips of the fingers of his left hand, a delightful continental gesture meaning "*!?-/× !§, we nearly lost it then!" Due to complete and uncontrollable front-end break-away we eventually drove that car over the edge of a mountain, but that is another story.

Returning to our first condition where "unwinding" the steering gives greater feeling of control; this is why we see Brooks or Salvadori on an Aston Martin DB3S take a corner with a great amount of steering lock, under stable conditions, but if the front-end breaks away you will see them "unwind" the steering a little until the component F returns to the maximum. If you see a driver holding his understeering car, such as the DB3S, on a constant amount of steering lock it is self-evident that he is not at the maximum value of C_f. On the other hand, when you see a driver apply steering lock and then go straight ahead on to the grass, you have seen F maximum reached and passed so quickly that the human reflexes have not been up to the situation. To see real artistry with an understeering car is to see the driver apply more and more lock as he enters the corner and then reach a point where he reduces this lock, not beyond the centre line of the steering lock, for that would mean that some other conditions had come into play and the car had changed from under to oversteer, or referring to Fig. 24 the point M had been reached, but at a lesser amount of lock than when entering the corner. By reason of his natural senses, vision and the torque he is applying to the steering wheel to overcome the natural corrective force of the front tyres, our skilful driver can let the car run in an arc towards the outside of the corner in one long curve continually around the breakaway point of the front tyres. As soon as the front tyres begin to have reduced radial force he increases it by reducing the steering lock. It is, of course, assumed that he has all the other requisites to judge whether the road is wide enough and the corner of such a radius as to allow this. As mentioned earlier, such corners as Abbey Curve at Silverstone and Fordwater at Goodwood are particularly suited to this driving style. A sharp corner, such as a right-angle or hairpin does not encourage this method. Many drivers like this understeer characteristic under extremes of cornering force, but it does put a limit on the overall ability of car and driver, for if he should make a mistake and enter the corner too fast his only way out is to run wide in an endeavour to retain control and this will take him on to the grass on an airfield circuit, or into a ditch or brick wall on a road circuit. British racing circuits, due to their habit of being in wide-open spaces, tend to encourage these handling characteristics, which is one reason why the introduction of the "tight" little Crystal Palace circuit caused such alarm and despondency to begin with.

At this stage, although we are considering the understeering car, it is worth digressing to notice that very skilful drivers can make use of the effects already described to counteract deficiencies of cars with considerable final oversteer. If the front-end cornering power of the oversteering car can be reduced below that of the back end, then the car will understeer: a reversal of that described with the $3\frac{1}{2}$-litre Maserati. This can be done in practice by rotating the vector F backwards to such an angle that its useful cornering component F_c is very small. Either by jerking the steering on to considerable lock or by turning it whilst braking hard, the front-end can be made to break-away prematurely, and it will stay in this condition provided the steering angle is not removed and the car does not slow up too much. This process is aided by the transient effects connected with the polar moment of inertia of the car on entering a corner, but these we need not deal with here. It is difficult to decide who first applied this method of inducing understeer when desirable, but it is certain that the immortal Nuvolari appreciated the desirability as long ago as 1930–32, though it is unlikely that he knew the technical reasons why. He came to the conclusion by intuition, and it explains why he was often seen on a fast bend with his wheels pointing into a corner, while his contemporaries on identical cars would have the tail sliding outwards. Whether he achieved this condition by running on low tyre pressures in the front, jerking the steering wheel to induce break-away on the front tyres, or using the brakes at the critical moment, I could not say, but he certainly had a remarkable ability for producing understeer on cars that by design had inherent oversteer.

I have had personal experience of this practice when being driven by Stirling Moss in Porsche and Mercedes-Benz cars. On my own Porsche with standard tyres, oversteer is built-in and similarly the 300SL is a fundamentally oversteering car, but in both vehicles I have had illustrations of provoking understeer on a long fast bend by jerking the steering wheel on to considerable lock at the critical point when going into a corner. It looked easy enough but when I came to try it myself I found numerous pitfalls. Firstly, to reach break-away on any of the cars involved meant cornering at very high values of C_f, i.e. the speed and/or curvature of the corner were considerable, and I found my estimation of the limit hopelessly below what it actually was. Secondly I was never brave enough to turn the steering wheel more than seemed reasonable for the radius of the corner, for obviously, if the oversteering 300SL was going to be turned into an understeerer the front tyres would have to be forced into generating greater slip-angles than the rear ones and the inherent feel of the car was to present the opposite conditions; also, to make the front angles greater meant approaching the break-away point of the front tyres and that involved speeds and judgment a bit beyond my abilities. After demonstrating this situation on a very fast "works" 300SL Moss tried to "teach me" on a 220S Mercedes-Benz, which had an understeer anyway, by making me deliberately apply too much understeer and reach break-away on the front tyres. As I drove into a corner he would yell, "More lock; now!" If I responded we achieved a spectacular understeer drift, using all the road and maintaining our speed round the corner. If I did not respond, as often happened to begin with, the car lost speed due to tyre scrub and we cornered in a jerky and untidy fashion. However, I am glad to say that I eventually conquered this technique, albeit only for low cornering forces as generated by my very standard Porsche. I know full well that I could never be brave enough to achieve this situation with a 300SL, let alone a Grand Prix car. This is a very dodgy condition to induce, for when the artificial understeer stops the car will turn into an oversteer very violently, for we are around the portion G on our line O_1—D in Fig. 24, but a really brilliant driver will put this action to good use.

To make this more easy to appreciate let me recount another experience with Stirling Moss. I must apologise to the fans of other great drivers but it so happens that circumstances have provided me with more factual data with Moss at the wheel than other drivers, but you can just as well read Fangio, Behra, Hawthorn, Brooks instead of Moss, for any Grand Prix lap record-holder must be capable of indulging in these limits of high-speed driving, though some are more adept at them than others.

The car in question was a 300SL Mercedes-Benz, a wicked and vicious final-oversteering monster, and Moss was practising for the 1955 Targa Florio. I arrived on the scene just as he was setting off for another lap on the open roads and he offered me a ride which I was quick to accept, before someone else beat me to it. I did not know the course at all, so looked forward with interest and anticipation and, knowing the oversteer handling characteristic of the 300SL, I prepared myself for certain eventualities. Imagine my surprise when we went into a sharp right-hand corner and Moss provoked the most violent understeer by going into the corner much faster than would be reasonable and putting on violent right-hand lock (A). I was not actually frightened but I remember thinking, "Crikey, what the devil does he think he is doing?" The situation was as illustrated in Fig. 28, though I have shown an exposed-wheel racing car for the sake of clarity, but I had no idea the road turned sharp left after the right-hand corner, though Moss obviously knew this, having learnt the circuit.

Now it is quite obvious that if you provoke understeer on a car that has a natural desire to oversteer you are going to get into difficul-

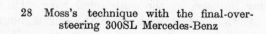

28   Moss's technique with the final-over-steering 300SL Mercedes-Benz

ties when your artificial understeer stops, as it must when the steering is unwound at the end of the corner, and when that happens the tail of the car is going to whip round very suddenly so that the driver will need all his powers of anticipation and reflex to cope with the situation. Knowing this I thought that Moss had gone mad in provoking violent understeer on the 300SL at the speed we were travelling, so I just resigned myself to another accident. As the car slid through the corner and lost momentum (B) we reached a point in the middle of the road (C) when he straightened up the steering and then immediately turned it again, his movements coinciding exactly with the change of direction of the car as the artificial understeer ran out and the normal characteristic of the car took charge (D). At that point we were nicely placed for the left-hand bend and the car went round it in a delightful oversteer slide and we accelerated away up the succeeding straight (E). As I realised what had happened, my only thought was, "Oh dear, I could never hope to drive like that, he really is a genius."

The interesting thing is that these top-drivers do all this sort of thing without any knowledge of the theory behind their movements. They rely solely on initial trial and error, experience and their beautifully adjusted natural faculties which we have already dealt with. To be driven by them under such conditions makes you really appreciate their artistry, and the fact that real genius is born and not made.

Before we leave this particular matter it is worth digressing yet again on to the subject of sidecar racing and the business of being a passenger, for what Moss did through the bends in Fig. 28 was very akin to movements that the racing sidecar passenger has to undergo. When a sidecar outfit takes a corner, either to right or left, the centrifugal force set up tries to upset the stability and the job of the passenger is to put his weight where it will counteract the turning moment being imposed by the centrifugal force. On the left-hand bends this force tries to turn the outfit about the contact areas of the wheels of the motor-cycle, and on right-hand bends, about the front wheel of the machine, and the wheel of the sidecar; this applies to a sidecar mounted on the left, for a sidecar mounted on the right the opposite conditions apply. In Fig. 4, I am seen leaning out of a sidecar on a fast right-hand bend counteracting the effect of centrifugal force, which is acting through the centre of gravity of the whole outfit, somewhere just below the level of the bottom of the petrol tank, and which is trying to rotate the machine about the contact area of the front and rear tyres. By leaning out as illustrated I am doing two things: firstly my weight moves the effective centre of gravity in towards the corner, and reduces the turning moment, and secondly it lowers the effective centre of gravity, which has the same effect. Now at no time can a passenger get too low, for the lower the total centre of gravity the less the tendency for the outfit to overturn, but he can lean out too far. The ideal situation is when the sidecar wheel is only just making contact with the ground but with virtually no pressure on the road, for that way tyre scrub is minimized as the wheel does not steer. The passenger is very conscious of the centrifugal force acting on his body and trying to push him back into the sidecar and it is this force that he has to resist by pushing himself out at right-angles to the machine. As you go into a corner you press yourself outwards, against the centrifugal force, and it is a simple matter to feel when this force reaches a maximum value, indicating that the tyres of the outfit are generating the maximum side-thrust, or our aforementioned value F has reached its highest point.

Once past the apex of the corner the centrifugal force will begin to diminish and this is the critical point at which a passenger can either make life hard or easy for himself. As the outfit begins to straighten up towards the end of the curve about which it is cornering, the passenger can relax slightly and let the centrifugal force propel him back into the sidecar, and if he is clever he can anticipate the diminishing force and slide easily inwards with very little physical effort. It is a rapid action and counter-action movement, as the corner decreases the centrifugal force decreases, and in consequence there is no need for the centre of gravity to

151

be so far in towards the centre of the corner, so the passenger need not be leaning out so much. A passenger with good feel will slide smoothly back into the sidecar at exactly the same rate as the centrifugal force is diminishing, so that by the time the outfit is running straight again he is lying prone in the sidecar. If you do not do this it means that you have to strain against the centrifugal force unnecessarily, and if you remain leaning out until the outfit is straight, you then have to expend energy in lifting the dead-weight of your body back into the sidecar. Of course, if you let centrifugal force throw you back into the sidecar too soon, the wheel will lift and upset the rider's equilibrium and you'll soon hear about that! It is quite remarkable the number of people who ride as passengers who do not appreciate this business of letting centrifugal force assist you, and they are easy to pick out for they invariably finish a race with aching arm muscles due to the physical effort of lifting their weight after each corner.

While the foregoing merely explains how to make passengering easier it has a more important application, and this is when you take an Ess-bend at high speed. The good passenger will always be a fraction ahead of the actual movement of the outfit and, if he is, then the rider will not feel his movements affecting the machine, but will only be conscious of the results, which will be equilibrium. Some riders are not sensitive enough to notice this but the good ones are, just as good car drivers are very sensitive, and Eric Oliver tried lots of passengers who would always "rock the boat" as he put it. Returning to our Ess-bend at, say, 85 m.p.h. and high cornering powers: there would not be time for the passenger to move from leaning fully out of the sidecar to leaning over the rear wheel of the motor-cycle if there was no centrifugal force to help him. I have tried measuring the time taken to move from one side to the other when stationary and it is more than that taken for the outfit to change direction at very high cornering powers, so the only way for the passenger to move more quickly is to relax at the exact moment when centrifugal force will throw him across the outfit ready for the second part of the Ess. A perfect example of this is provided by the bends after the start on the Spa circuit, or nearer home, the uphill "left-and-right" leading into Clearways bend at Brands Hatch. Naturally not all riders can produce the skill necessary to reach the high cornering power required for this instance, but if he can then his passenger must use the centrifugal force or he will lag behind. It is easy for a quick passenger to ride for a slow rider, but the reverse is impossible.

Now, to return to Stirling Moss in his 300SL in Fig. 28, a similar situation presented itself, namely that of changing the direction of the car in an Ess-bend at a higher rate than is possible by normal physical means, i.e. by use of the steerable front wheels. He achieved the greater rate-of-change of direction by using the inherent oversteer characteristic of the car at precisely the correct moment, just as the passenger used the centrifugal force to speed up his physically limited rate-of-change. Had Moss taken the first part of the corner on a natural oversteer the car would not have flicked round the other way when he wanted it too, and the only way he could have achieved that would have been by a gross reduction of speed, and by steering-wheel movement, which would have produced a slower overall cornering speed. This sort of driving technique calls for a car with final oversteer and also one that will respond adequately to the provocation of understeer, while it goes without saying that the driver must be exceptionally highly skilled or the characteristics of the car will be wasted on him. Such a manœuvre as I have described would be exceedingly dangerous if it were not carried out properly, so that a final understeer characteristic is more desirable for the average driver like you and me. I would suggest that if any reader is disposed to try this technique he finds a wide open space and does not use a car with a high centre of gravity, or he will find himself on his roof.

This induced understeer technique is essentially for driving at the maximum cornering force and the top Grand Prix drivers use this theory in two further ways. One is to get them out of trouble if they enter a corner too fast, and the other is to take a corner at over the reasonable limit, when trying for a lap record. If, due to the use of his mental faculties, a driver realises he is approaching a corner too fast he will apply steering lock into the corner very sharply. This has the effect of causing the front tyres to reach break-away and the resultant frictional component causes the car to lose speed. In order to return steering control the driver must "unwind" the steering, which reduces the slowing-up

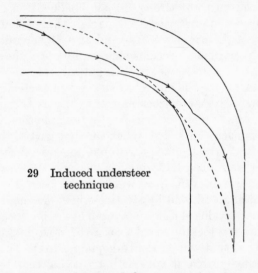

29   Induced understeer
technique

process of the tyre frictional forces, so that he must once again apply more lock, and so on until the corner is ended. The path of a car under such extreme conditions is shown in Fig. 29 by the solid line, the broken line being the path the car should have taken had the approach speed not been too high. Most of the top drivers use this method for getting out of difficulties, and Tony Brooks once described it rather nicely in an article in a motoring journal by saying that he preferred a car that could be made to understeer because, if he made a mistake, he could cover up by the aforementioned method, and the spectators did not realise he had made the mistake as the car looked reasonably stable. If this is not

154

done, and the normal oversteer is allowed to take charge, a mistake in the approach speed meant taking the corner in a full-opposite lock slide which was untidy and obviously wrong. While this final remark is not strictly true, as we shall see very shortly, the first remark is valid.

Now, I have tried this method deliberately in my Porsche car on an open bend with loose edges, and found it comparatively simple to do around speeds of 50–60 m.p.h. and the lower cornering powers of which a Porsche is capable when compared to a Grand Prix car. When I tried to visualise applying the same technique at 150 m.p.h. or much higher values of C_f, then I realised my personal driving limitations and became very appreciative of the abilities of the Grand Prix drivers who can drive to such limits. If a racing driver can apply this technique to his car he can take certain fast corners in this manner deliberately, and if he is really skilled at it he can achieve a fractionally higher overall speed through the corner. It means that he can brake a little later entering the corner at a higher speed, and also leave the corner at the same speed as if he had taken it on a constant understeer just below break-away point. Referring to Fig. 29 again— the solid line: due to road conditions he can usually manage two changes of direction before he reaches the edge of the available road at the end of the corner. If he is really determined about starting this series of movements he can get in three changes of movement, and Moss reckons to be able to achieve this deliberately. It is a technique he applies when trying for a lap record, especially on circuits such as Goodwood or Silverstone. Naturally, when he is driving on this very fine limit around the break-away point of the front tyres, it will be appreciated that the safety margin is very small, so that a minute error of judgment in either the approach speed or the moment for reducing steering lock would mean a helpless front-wheel slide into the *décor*. When we realise that the increase in approach speed to go from understeer near to the limit to understeer on the limit may only be 2 m.p.h. at a speed of 120 m.p.h., we can begin to appreciate the remarkable finesse required to drive in this manner, and we will also realise that though such characteristics of car and driver would give us the highest cornering power, for given conditions, it is at the expense of "no way out" once the limit is passed, other than a crash. This is why I said earlier that final understeer was not desirable for the overall picture, though it is helpful on fast open bends.

CHAPTER XII

OVERSTEER

WE are now seeing some of the ways in which a top racing driver differs from the ordinary, everyday, good driver, and we have seen that if our driver is extremely competent we can give him a car with final oversteer. Now if we give theoretical consideration to final oversteer we will see that it is possible for a handful of drivers in the World Champion category to exploit this characteristic in search of the ultimate in cornering speed, but the limits are so fine that I would not have thought it possible had I not witnessed it happening.

In considering the final oversteering car we will direct our attention to the back wheels, since it is here, by definition of oversteer, that the break-away point is first reached and the speed of the car round a corner therefore limited. If there is no braking or driving force being applied to the rear wheels, only the component F_c in Fig. 30 is available to counteract centrifugal force. As break-away occurs, ϕ_r increases and consequently F_c diminishes, so that the car goes with increasing rapidity into a spin. Now if we apply a propulsive force P, the vector F is swung round until, if P is the right value, F is directed towards the centre of curvature, as shown in the inset to Fig. 30. Therefore, by well-judged use of the throttle to provide power at the rear wheels (always assuming there is a sufficient surplus of power available) the car which is about to spin may be brought back under control, and the maximum cornering force regained. If too much power is applied then the vector F will be swung too far forwards, beyond the line of F_c, so that the cornering force will diminish again and the car will spin off as it originally tried to do.

157

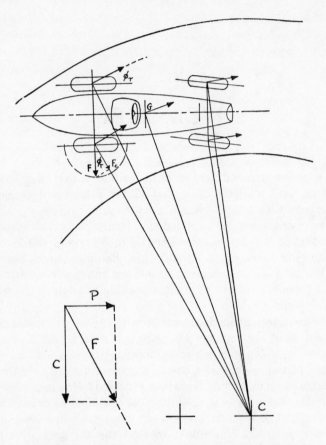

30   Forces acting on an oversteering car in a corner

Furthermore the conditions are not the same for the two rear wheels, for weight transference will put most of the load on the outer wheel and, if an ordinary free differential is built into the rear axle, it is likely that quite moderate power transmission will spin the inside wheel.   If the car is on the limit of cornering power this will lead to real trouble, for the spinning wheel will virtually have zero cornering power and the action of the differential will mean that no driving force is going into the outside wheel, so that the overall cornering

158

power of the two rear wheels will be suddenly and drastically reduced, which will cause a violent oversteer tendency and the car will spin round. The only way in which this power application technique can be applied is when the car is fitted with restricted-slip differential of the ZF type, or in unusual designs having very small weight transference at the rear wheels.

After we had considered the case of a car with front-end break-away, we saw that the theory could be applied to driving a car with rear-end break-away, and similarly the previous paragraph can be of importance with a car having final understeer as cited in the case of the 1956 Maserati $3\frac{1}{2}$-litre earlier on. The application of too much throttle reduces the cornering power of the rear tyres to match that of the front tyres and the car is balanced accordingly. However, there is an important and fundamental difference in the two cases for, by reducing the cornering power of the rear tyres, we are bringing the rear-end C_f down to the lower level of the front-end, whereas the driver who can balance his oversteering car on the throttle is raising the rear-end cornering ability to that of the front-end and attaining the highest level at both ends.

As I have said, this theory seemed sound enough but I doubted whether mere human beings could develop so fine a sense of touch as to be able to achieve power-control of the rear-end cornering ability in practice, and it seemed unlikely that present day Formula I Grand Prix cars would have a sufficient surplus of power anyway. However, over the past few years it has become possible for this theory to be put into practice, and the first time I saw it was in 1955 with the W196 Mercedes-Benz. It was rather interesting how this came about, for it was a chance conversation between Moss and one of his team-mates in the Mercedes-Benz team that prompted me to follow up the subject. They were discussing a 100 m.p.h. bend, and Moss was maintaining that the W196 took it in a long oversteer, which was perfectly correct, and that when he reached the limit of adhesion he put his foot hard on the throttle in order to prevent losing the tail

159

of the car completely, this action bringing the rear more in line with the front, so that he ended the corner on full throttle with the tail no longer sliding outwards, even though he had started the corner on a light throttle with the tail sliding outwards. His team-mate was rather incredulous about this, and had it been anyone but Moss he would have called him a liar on the spot, for he maintained that when *he* reached the limit on the rear wheels he lifted his foot from the throttle and the tail came in again. Obviously one of them was wrong, and after a time it became clear that the two drivers had different ideas about what was the limit of adhesion of the rear wheels. What was more interesting was the fact that Moss was obviously reaching break-away point on the rear tyres, whereas his companion was some two or three degrees below break-away, and due to his lower sensitivity he only *thought* he was at maximum cornering force. At the lower cornering force which he considered the limit, lifting his foot from the throttle would merely increase the drag-component of the cornering force and slow the car down, so that application of steering lock would bring the tail inwards. However, if this driver had reached the maximum cornering force and had still insisted on lifting his foot, then the tail would have swung viciously outwards and spun him off on to the grass as we have seen. With Moss at the wheel the car would have maintained equilibrium on the point of break-away and, if a delicate foot was used to control the forward thrust, the corner could be completed, still on the limit of cornering power.

Now all the foregoing was dependent on the W196 having sufficient power, relative to its cornering ability and weight, to provide the necessary forward thrust at 100 m.p.h., and discussing the subject later on with Director Rudolf Uhlenhaut of the Daimler-Benz racing department, I learnt that this was quite possible. When I told him about Moss getting out of trouble by the application of power under such circumstances, he was agreeably surprised and told me that Fangio applied the same technique. He went on to say that the car had been deliberately designed with a handling characteristic that ended in final oversteer for just this reason. He told me that though they designed the car to react in this manner at the time, he never thought there would be a racing driver capable of (a) reaching the cornering limit of the car on a very fast bend and (b) having the ability to apply power in the required manner in order to maintain control. He was exceedingly pleased to know that his two best drivers were able to use the W196 to its fullest extent on fast corners. We discussed the handling characteristic curve O_1—B illustrated in Fig. 24, and the one for the W196 was very similar to the theoretical one I have shown, with the exception that the Mercedes-Benz had rather more understeer at lower cornering forces, and Uhlenhaut said that they hoped to be able to reduce it for 1956, but alas they had to stop their experiments at the end of 1955 when the Daimler-Benz directors decreed "no more racing".

Continuing this matter further I then asked Moss whether he had ever been able to apply this technique to any other racing car, but it transpired that he had not, and the 1954 Maserati 250F, although it had similar handling characteristics, did not have a sufficient reserve of power, so in consequence it could not be driven so close to the limit of cornering power as its German rival. At that time Ferrari was still using the Super Squalo, which as we have seen had the wrong characteristics anyway for this technique—which was, perhaps, just as well as it certainly would not have had enough power. The Lancia D50 in those days was designed very much on a neutral-steer principle, so it too did not enter into the matter. In 1956, however, Ferrari altered the handling of the Lancia to one of final oversteer, and many times during that season I saw Fangio and Collins get themselves out of oversteer trouble by applying power, albeit on slowish corners of less than 100 m.p.h. In 1957 the 250F Maserati became amenable to this power technique, more by luck than judgment, for it had had final oversteer characteristics all its life, but had previously suffered from insufficient power and too much weight. The "works" lightweight cars in 1957, running on nitro-methane, developed sufficient power to have a reserve on fast corners and throughout the season Fangio gave some wonderful demonstrations of cornering with the rear wheels held on breakaway on fast corners at 100 m.p.h. or more, by using the throttle. I watched him closely on the bend before the pits at Rouen, which was fast and smooth and ideal for this technique, and you could see the car increasing its attitude-angle to the corner (i.e. developing very large slip-angles), and then at the crucial moment he would apply power and hold the car in a long slide through the corner. It is worth mentioning here that for maximum forward thrust a small amount of tyre slip is necessary, this being due to a phenomenon connected with the constructional properties of the tyre, so that Fangio would leave the corner with the tyres leaving black marks on the road, but under full directional control. On a few occasions I saw him overdo this application of power and the tail snaked viciously, demanding instantaneous steering correction and in lesser hands the car would have spun round.

Jean Behra also employed this technique on occasions, more especially to get himself out of a difficult situation after he had entered a corner too fast, whereas Fangio was doing it deliberately to attain the maximum cornering power from his car. At the end of the 1957 season when the V12-cylinder Maserati Grand Prix car began to show promise, Behra utilised this technique (31), for this car had more than enough power to be effective, and many were the demonstrations the Frenchman gave on the South Curve at Monza during the Italian Grand Prix.

The Lancia/Ferraris had been redesigned and had too much understeer in 1957, and the British cars such as Connaught, Vanwall and B.R.M. were also unable to be used for this technique, as they all possessed inherent final understeer, and/or insufficient power.

From the foregoing we can now see that Fangio, Moss, Behra and company, when power-sliding their corners, were merely altering the tail end of the handling-characteristic curve about the point G in Fig. 24, or in other words

31 During 1957 the V12-cylindered Grand Prix Maserati proved to have the right characteristics of power and handling for the driver to be able to reduce oversteer by the application of the right amount of throttle. Behra is seen at Monza with this car, preventing the rear wheels from sliding further out by opening the throttle at the precise moment necessary to retain stability

32 A perfect illustration of understeer and oversteer providing the same cornering power during the 1957 Italian Grand Prix at Monza. Moss leads in an understeering Vanwall, then comes Behra in a power-controlled oversteer, followed by Brooks in another Vanwall also understeering, Fangio in a 6-cylinder Maserati in a similar attitude to Behra and Lewis-Evans completing the understeer trio of Vanwalls. The two makes are typical of the British and Continental views on handling characteristics.

prolonging the natural tendency of the car at maximum cornering forces. As I remarked earlier, final oversteer was considered desirable by some designers as it allowed the driver an added safety margin, providing he was skilful enough, whereas final understeer had no easy way out once the limit was reached. With modern knowledge of tyre construction and adhesion properties, which after all are the limiting factors in cornering power of a racing car, and also modern knowledge of suspension which keeps the tyre in contact with the road, there are very few human beings able to reach the maximum cornering force that the modern Grand Prix car can withstand, especially at speeds around 120–160 m.p.h. Designing a racing car with continuous understeer means that the *average* racing driver can achieve quite high cornering powers with complete safety and the car can have consistent characteristics. If the car is designed with a combination of initial understeer and final oversteer it will not show any particular advantage in the hands of the average racing driver, and many would find the change from one condition to the other tiresome, but given a *maestro* such as any of the small handful of men at the top of Grand Prix racing, then such a car, providing of course it has a sufficient reserve of power, could be exploited to the full and achieve higher cornering powers than its opposite number.

Earlier I mentioned the desirability of oversteer on sharp corners, and now we can see why. Even on a hairpin we can get our first-class driver to apply very high cornering forces, which brings our handling into the oversteer part of our Fig. 24, and this means that the tail can be swung outwards round the bend, controlled by the throttle, and the car will leave the corner with full forward thrust on the rear wheels. Our understeering car if cornered at the maximum on a hairpin will tend to run outwards at the front, and any application of power to the rear wheels will only increase this undesirable condition, so that the driver cannot apply full power until after the corner and the car is pointing straight again. Watching the W196 Mercedes-Benz and the 1957 "works" Maseratis on a hairpin corner gave ample indication of the cornering forces being utilised by various drivers. The top drivers would take the corner with the tail swinging outwards, while a timid driver would actually have a degree of understeer showing, his speed round the hairpin generating a very low cornering force.

Before leaving this subject, and we have only touched on the surface in reality, there are two small but vital points to be added. On a fast corner of over 100 m.p.h. for example, when the driver reaches break-away and applies a forward thrust by opening the throttle, there is a further small gain assisting the increase of the radial component of the rear wheels which is resisting centrifugal force. This is caused by the action of fore-and-aft weight-transference brought about by providing an acceleration to the car as a whole. When a car is accelerated by a thrust at the back wheels, there is a slight change of weight distribution, the rear wheels having an increase of effective load at the expense of a diminution at the front wheels. This means that the maximum sidethrust of the front tyres is reduced, for we know that F is equal to the weight carried multiplied by the coefficient of friction, so that a reduction in W must mean a reduction in F, the coefficient of friction being constant. This reduction of F for the front wheels will mean an increase of the slip-angle, the radial velocity getting greater rather than smaller, which will tend to encourage an understeer effect on the car. At the same time, the increase of W for the rear wheels will help to keep the F value for them at its maximum, so that all the effects from the application of power at break-away work towards maintaining stability or preventing the oversteer getting out of control. On the W196 Mercedes-Benz there was also an added bonus, for this car had a low-pivot swing-axle layout at the rear, with positive camber to the wheels. The weight transference under a forward thrust increased this camber angle, which assisted the cornering power of the tyres. While the effect of this was minute, at least any geometrical movement of the suspension due to weight transference was in a helpful direction rather than an opposing one, as on some systems, or a neutral one as with de Dion rear suspension.

Although in general practice a car with a power-to-weight ratio of a Grand Prix car is needed to utilise this power cornering technique at the limit, it has proved possible with other cars, and the factory Porsche Spyders with their low-pivot rear swing-axles have proved amenable to it, naturally at lower cornering speeds than with Grand Prix cars. Given the appropriate handling characteristics, the present-day Formula II cars could also be driven in this manner, but as a rule British designers favour total understeer, in direct opposition to German designers who tend towards final oversteer characteristic. It is rather interesting that during the past ten years, during which time the science of road-holding has been applied to competition cars, the British and German designers have supported these opposing views, almost to the point of each becoming a national trait (32). We must not think for a moment that all this roadholding and suspension knowledge is recent, for it has been known in theory for many years, and American car designers have been fully conversant with it all since the mid-1930's, but it is only over the past ten years that so much of this latent knowledge has been applied to competition cars with such conclusive results being so plainly visible. The normal passenger car as used on the road may have ideal characteristics but is never driven to the limit, so that its true character remains hidden. However, club racing with production cars, rallies and so on, have made a great change, and the handling limits of almost every production car have long since been reached and passed, and many of them were found very badly wanting.

CHAPTER XIII

INSTINCTS

IN the previous chapter we have seen the reasons why a racing driver does things, and before that we examined the physical attributes that allowed him to take various actions and we have traced the physical and mental processes which operate when he is driving very close to the limits of safety. We should by now have a certain amount of respect for the racing driver, especially those at the top of the racing world and, in addition, we can appreciate that they are not entirely normal average human beings, but highly developed and very sensitive ones. Before we end our study of this special being let us return to the actual racing and the cars, and see how the drivers react to various conditions connected with the controls of the car.

All drivers have certain preferences for such things as steering wheels: one driver prefers four spokes to three; another is not bothered about the number of spokes, some like wooden-rimmed wheels of very thin section, other prefer thick plastic-covered wheels and so on. One of the items that produces a fair amount of discussion among drivers is the question of the pedals—clutch, brake and accelerator— and in particular their disposition relative to one another.

In early days, when all gearboxes were of the "crash" type, which is to say that the pinions had straight-cut teeth, and when there was no synchromesh mechanism to assist gearchanging, only the skill of the driver ensured that the speeds of the different pinions were synchronized while changing to a lower gear at the same time as applying the brakes, a method known as "heel-and-toe" gearchanging was developed which is still used by the more adept drivers even on normal touring cars, as an aid to easier and smoother driving. While cars were still being basically-designed and not assembled from a collection of components best arrayed to suit the salesman, the position of the control pedals received much thought. In order to change down with the "heel-and-toe" method, the ball of the right foot pressed firmly on the brake pedal, and when the time came to select a lower gear and the need to synchronise the gearbox pinions arose it was a simple matter to continue pressing the brake with the ball of the right foot and at the same time hinge the foot about the ankle and, with the heel, press the accelerator and speed up the gearbox internals, suitable movements having been made with the gearlever and clutch pedal, of course. When sitting in a normal posture, and assuming the driver is of normal build, the toes tend to turn outwards, so that an ideal place for the brake pedal was on the right of the accelerator pedal. Thus could the "heel-and-toe" changing method be used without any contortions of the foot other than a simple hinging about the ankle joint.

Cars born from a sporting parenthood invariably adopted this pedal layout, especially through the Vintage years of the 1920's, good examples being Alfa Romeo and Bugatti, while on racing cars it was practically universal. With the advent of synchromesh gearboxes on touring cars the use of the accelerator in conjunction with the brake, or for that matter at all, when making downward changes, became unnecessary and the accelerator pedal moved over to the right of the brake pedal so that the feet took up a normal splayed-out attitude when resting on accelerator and clutch pedals. Italian racing cars have continued to use the old method of a central accelerator pedal, for even though the gearboxes today have quick, easy dog-clutch engagement making double-declutching not absolutely necessary, it is considered kinder to the mechanism to use the accelerator during downward changes. In consequence the "heel-and-toe" method is still used by racing drivers, and Maserati and Ferrari have the accelerator pedal to the left of the brake pedal. Oddly enough, the W196 Mercedes-Benz had it on the right of the brake pedal, but in order to facilitate "heel-and-toe" changing the accelerator had a sideways extension which projected towards the brake pedal, the driver's foot making the hinged ankle movement with the foot virtually pointing straight upwards.

The point of all the foregoing is to show that pedal layout by no means follows a universal plan, and there are some drivers who refuse to drive a car with the accelerator on the left of the brake pedal, or as it is referred to, "central throttle pedal layout". These drivers use the conventional right-mounted accelerator pedal in their normal touring cars, probably learnt to drive on just such an arrangement, and accordingly think that they have conditioned their foot muscular reflexes to this layout, any alteration of pedal placing calling for conscious thought when using the pedals. As we have seen, unconscious reactions play a major part in the movements of a driver when travelling at high speeds, so that anything that might lead to a faulty foot movement is quite rightly to be avoided.

Two classic incidents come to mind on this matter of "getting the feet crossed", one serious, the other not— though it could have been. The German driver Wolfgang von Trips was practising at the Nürburgring with a sports Ferrari, fitted with central throttle layout, and he was driving very much on reflex actions, having an intimate knowledge of the difficult circuit. The Ferrari team-manager wanted to try out a *Gran Turismo* Europa Ferrari, and when von Trips got out of the sports Ferrari he was asked to put in some laps with the *Gran Turismo* car. Now this 3-litre coupé was very nearly as fast as the open sports Ferrari, but being a production model it had the accelerator on the right of the brake pedal; in other words, the conventional production layout. The German driver set off at virtually the same sort of speeds he had been doing in the sports car and all went well until he got to a difficult downhill section, when he automatically relied on his reflexes and approaching a sharp left-hand turn he trod on the accelerator instead of the brake pedal. It was a simple question of the natural angle of the feet when sitting at the driving wheel; his muscular control positioned his foot for braking and pressed in the appropriate place, but the wrong pedal was there. The result was a rather serious crash that put von Trips out of racing for nearly a whole season, and which might easily have caused his death. Now, the interesting thing is that he drives touring cars on the public roads with a normal pedal layout and doesn't make mistakes, and equally, he doesn't make mistakes when he gets from his production touring car into the Ferrari racing cars, even though the pedal disposition is reversed. The whole environment of the racing car is so different that a great number of reflexes have to be either modified or sharpened up, so that surrounded as he is by the racing machinery he reacts one way, whereas in the comparative silence and comfort of a touring car he reacts the opposite way with no difficulty. The *Gran Turismo* car in which he crashed had been prepared for racing, and the noise, feel, seating position and surroundings were very similar to the open sports Ferrari he had just left; also, he was driving on the same closed racing circuit, under the same conditions, and for all practical purposes at the same speed, so that it was not surprising that his reflexes went on reacting to their "racing" stimulus, which resulted in a bad crash.

I have not dealt with this incident at such length in order to justify von Trips' crash, but to illustrate how easy it is for the racing driver to be lulled into difficult and dangerous situations.

The other incident concerns Stirling Moss at Barcelona in 1954, when he was driving his own Grand Prix Maserati as part of the factory team. His own car had been specially built for him and had the accelerator on the right of the brake pedal, for he learnt to drive with that layout and refuses to alter his technique, rightly believing it to be an unnecessary source of possible danger, as we have seen with the von Trips incident. During practice at Barcelona there was an opportunity to try one of the factory Maseratis, but it had a central throttle layout. However, for once Moss relented on his pedal ruling and tried the car, being all the while very conscious that he had to turn his foot outwards for the brake pedal. By not letting his reflexes take complete control he accomplished a number of laps quite satisfactorily, until he was going into a bend with another competitor in front of him. The other car got into a skid and Moss had to take avoiding action at very short notice. Under normal circumstances it is possible to be aware of a dangerous reflex like this and consciously prevent its occurrence, as Moss had been doing, but in times of crisis it is another matter, and this was just such an occasion. He had to put the Maserati into a deliberate slide in order to avoid the other car, and all was going well until he reached the point where he wanted to check the slide and change the direction of his car. It was apparent to him that a sharp jab on the brakes was required, and being in a Grand Prix Maserati his muscular reflexes moved his foot as required, but of course it was the accelerator he jabbed. Although he immediately stabbed again and hit the right pedal it was too late, the car had accelerated forward and hit a tree head-on, fortunately with no very serious damage. When you realise that the time taken to move the foot from the wrong pedal to the right one could only amount to a very small fraction of a second, yet in that time the car got beyond the driver's control, you will realise to what very close limits the racing driver is driving. Moss did not need any convincing about the undesirability of driving a car with reversed pedal layout, and all his better judgment had told him he should not have done it, but his enthusiasm to try a factory Maserati got the better of his judgment, with very nearly disastrous results. It was a similar case to von Trips' crash —a case of being in the same environment and under the same conditions—but in fact even more understandable when two Grand Prix Maseratis were involved.

At first sight this poses the question: "Why build racing cars with different pedal layouts?" There really is no justification, except that some drivers prefer the central throttle layout on a racing car that they intend to drive to

172

the limit and in which they utilize the "heel-and-toe" method of gearchanging. Many of them can drive with either layout, and if questioned on the subject will shrug the shoulders and say it's all the same to them; they really have no preference for pedal layout. Naturally this leaves the choice to the designer, and if he has been designing racing cars only, and for a long time, the chances are he will use the old original central throttle layout. Both Fangio and Behra are of the easy-going type who will drive to the limit no matter what the throttle pedal position, while there are others who never really know, and when questioned will have to pause and think where the throttle is on a Ferrari or a Vanwall. Fangio gave an excellent illustration of his complete disregard for pedal positions in 1954 when he drove at Spa in the Belgian Grand Prix with a Maserati having a central throttle pedal, and won the race, which took place on Sunday. The following Wednesday he was at Rheims trying out the new W196 Mercedes-Benz for the first time, this German car having a right-handed throttle pedal, and on the Sunday after he won the Rheims race with the car. I am not going to say that he just gets in a car and goes fast, for when you see Fangio get into a new car you can see him make a quick appraisal of the layout of the controls, the pedals, the instruments, the gearlever, the rear-view mirrors and the petrol taps and magneto switches, all without making very much conscious movement; a peculiar characteristic of this great driver. Naturally if anything is badly placed he will criticise it, but if he gets from a car with a right-hand gearlever into a car with a left-hand lever, or with the pedal arrangement transposed, but with everything well placed, he can accept it as it is and drive fast with very little practice.

Most of the top-line Grand Prix drivers are like this, it all being part of the make-up of those who get to the top, but there are some who from personal prejudice or unfortunate experiences have little fads as regards pedals and controls. Briefly, drivers can be put into three categories: those who prefer a central throttle on a racing car with a crash gearbox, but drive a normal layout in road cars without question; those who insist on a right-hand throttle pedal on all cars; and those who can drive with any arrangement and can adapt themselves to any reasonable layout. Which category of driver is to be preferred is difficult to say, for the first have an obvious appreciation of the job in hand, the second are the careful type who will leave nothing to chance, and the third are obviously either carefree and reliant on their reflexes and skill, or they have a slight advantage of superior inborn fundamental characteristic very suitable for racing drivers. Personally I favour the third category of driver, as it rather indicates superior muscular coordination and a more flexible nervous system.

Another natural and instinctive decision a racing driver must take is the action to be followed when he has made a mistake and a crash is imminent. If he is approaching a sharp corner and he makes a mistake in his braking point, so that he is quite obviously arriving too fast for a normal passage through the corner, he has the choice of three alternatives. If there is an escape road, then the first choice is simple and he can use the emergency exit, but if there is no escape road then the second and third choices are difficult ones. He can either attempt to get round the corner, even though he knows he is going too fast for safety, or he can attempt to stop the car at all costs and ignore the corner completely. In this condition of acute emergency it is doubtful whether many drivers give any conscious thought to the matter at the time, most of them act on reflexes, and while they may previously have decided a plan of action for such an emergency, once the emergency arises drivers can be grouped into two categories—those who try to get round and those who try to stop.

If you watch drivers experimenting in practice you will soon see one arriving at a bend too fast, having experimented with the braking point until he has overstepped the limit. Then you will either see the maximum braking power being brought into play, with wheels locking momentarily as he seeks for the limit of retardation, and the car keeping a straight line in an endeavour to stop before using up the whole width of the approaching corner, or you will see an attempt to get round the corner in spite of the obvious knowledge that the speed is higher than the safe limit. In the first case the result is simple, the car either stops or it hits the border of the road, and if it is only a matter of straw bales then no more harm is done than a bending of the radiator cowling. If the driver is in the "try-to-corner-at-all-costs" group then the results can be much more complicated. A lot depends on the handling characteristics of the car in question. A Connaught, for example, with an inherent high degree of understeer will tend to slide its front wheels towards the outside of the bend and, if there is sufficient room, will hit the edge with its outside front wheel, or if there is a grass verge it will run off the road. In the case of an oversteering car, such as a Maserati, the chances are that it will spin once the driver has attempted to get round the corner, and will go off the road tail first, or strike the outer protection with the side of the car. If you can see Moss or Brooks, for example, you will find that they employ the technique of trying to get round the corner, but with an extra margin of chance added, which is the use of understeer to provide tyre scrub immediately their mistake is realised, in the same way as the method used for achieving an ultra-high lap speed which is illustrated in Fig. 29. This deliberate taking of a wrong line into the corner once it is realised that the car is going faster than intended before the corner, gives them a few more yards of road on which they can often find sufficient adhesion to regain control, or if it is inevitable that the car is going off the road it will mean that they leave the road at a lower speed than will the driver who merely tries to get round the corner on the correct line but at too high a speed.

I had a very lurid example of this action during the 1957 Mille Miglia in the 4·5-litre Maserati V8 with Moss. It was on the occasion when the brake pedal snapped off as he was slowing the car from 130 m.p.h. to 80–90 m.p.h. approaching a left-hand curve. As soon as he felt the brake pedal snap he forced the nose of the car in towards the corner, which produced violent understeer and we went round the corner teetering on the break-away point 15 m.p.h. faster than was intended and without any brakes. As he gave the steering its initial jerk on to left lock my thoughts were that he was taking his ultra-fast line into the corner, the type of line shown in Fig. 29, and I mentally reprimanded him for starting to "dice" so soon after the start, for we had only gone about seven miles. However, that thought was hardly over when I realised there was something amiss to cause him to do this, for our approach speed was higher than was reasonable even for Moss, and I realised he was working overtime to regain control. Fortunately he did so, and our brakeless 90 m.p.h. machine eventually came to rest. Had his natural instincts not made him take the emergency line into the corner, and had he not been practised in the art of slowing a car by means of its front tyres, he would have tried to get round the bend on the normal line and we should have suffered the most almighty crash on the outside of the corner. This was a wonderful example of experience saving our lives and is just one of the reasons why I have so much faith in the top drivers that I am prepared to be their passenger at Grand Prix speeds. To be able to sit by them while they put some sound theory into practice gives me enormous satisfaction. As I pointed out at the beginning of this book, there is nothing I'd like more than to be able to drive like a real Grand Prix driver, but having gone deeply into the theory behind their actions and having experienced these actions at close quarters, I know my personal limitations would not get me very far if I had to do the driving of a 400 b.h.p. sports car. What I should really enjoy would be to travel in a "single-seater" Grand Prix car with these very special racing drivers, when they are flirting with the ultimate in cornering ability.

It will be recalled that, when the late Onofre Marimon was killed at the Nürburgring, he went straight-on through a hedge. Now Marimon was definitely of the "try-and-stop-at-all-costs" group of drivers, and earlier that year I saw him arrive at a 90-degree bend bounded by straw bales much too fast, and as he was passing within a few feet of where I was standing I was able to observe that he made no attempt to get round the corner, but put all his concentration into stopping the car before it hit the straw bales, which on this occasion he was able to do.

What the driver's reaction to such a situation is depends a great deal on his anticipation, and how far ahead of his muscular responses it can work. It is obvious that a driver such as Moss or Brooks has a naturally sharp anticipation, which is why they can weigh-up the situation almost before it begins, and are able to start taking an avoiding action very early on. Because of this early anticipation their nervous processes and muscular responses are attuned accordingly and they can "play" with the car all the way through a slide, working always on the precept that there might be a change in road surface to effect adhesion, or the car might lose sufficient speed to regain adhesion, and by being continually on top of the situation their response is instantaneous; it is more than that, it can anticipate, and while this may only be measured as a tenth of a second, or even less, it is the difference between helpless "running out of road" and a piece of skilful recovery. Quite often this situation occurs and the onlooker has little or no idea that it is taking place, for the movement of the car under these circumstances is smooth and continuous. Naturally this can only be applied where the surrounding terrain allows; if you see it at Monte Carlo, for example, you can guarantee that the driver has lost control and is juggling between complete loss of control and recovery.

One rule that Eric Oliver and I made when we were side-car racing was that under no circumstances would we abandon ship. Jokingly we would say that even if the outfit was upside down we would hang on, for there was always a chance that it would right itself and we could go on racing. I can recall many occasions when we had to take to the grass verge during a road race, and only because we "kept stations" was Eric able to get the outfit back on the road again.

Knowing that he would never give up trying to regain control, it never crossed my mind to let go my hold and jump off, for I knew that that would be the end of all hope of continuing with the race, and after all our main object in those days was to race and win. After an excursion on to the grass, once we had the outfit back on an even keel, we would look at each other and grin, or stick our tongues out. After the race, while discussing the incident, for we always held a "post mortem" on the events of the day, Eric would say, "For a moment I was not sure who had control, me or the bicycle", or "I reckon we shared the control for a bit then." Delightful understatements, knowing full well that it was only luck that deflected the outfit in such a direction that he could regain full control. It was this sort of attitude that gave me such complete confidence to race with Eric, and I was rather pleased to find that Moss had the same outlook, when I raced with him in the Mille Miglia. After what we called a "dicey moment" we would look at each other and make a rude gesture, or put our tongues out, and when a driver can spontaneously react in this way to a brush with death, then I find it gives me enormous confidence in him. It is the driver who says nothing, or makes no movement after an obvious "incident", who frightens me into not going for another ride with him. It means that he has frightened himself, and as we have already discussed fright is a matter of the unknown. A driver who gets himself into unknown situations is a dangerous one. If a driver has time during an incident to become frightened then I maintain he has relaxed his concentration and is no longer keeping on top of the job in hand. I have sat beside many people when they have momentarily lost control of a car, and those who work away continuously, never giving up hope of regaining control, are those who get back on the road without being frightened. Those who suffer a nervous reaction get back on the road by sheer luck, or they crash completely.

178

CHAPTER XIV

MORALE

ALTHOUGH the chief object of a Racing Driver is to race, there are occasions when he is "still on duty" so to speak, though not actually driving or racing, and the way he reacts in such circumstances is very important. I have in mind at this moment those occasions when the car is at the pits, either for a routine refuelling stop or tyre change, or to have work done on the car due to some fault arising. Whatever the circumstances, whether they be premeditated or occasioned by an emergency, the behaviour of the driver is all-important, and he can have a strong effect on the pit staff, or his co-driver should it be in a long-distance event. If the pit-stop is a pre-arranged one, for refuelling or a change of tyres, some drivers are content to sit quietly while those concerned get on with their jobs, while others insist on keeping a close watch on what is going on, and even proffering help or words of encouragement, and such drivers are nothing short of a nuisance. You will find one driver sitting quite still in the cockpit, while another will be fussing about cleaning the windscreen, or trying to get a drink, or shouting for clean goggles. Invariably, a degree of pandemonium on the part of the driver is caused through bad planning, either on his part, or on the part of the team manager, for the driver knows before the race when he is likely to stop, and should have made arrangements for clean goggles, or a bottle of something to be available, while screen cleaning should be part of the mechanics' work and organised by the team-manager. Of course, there is no reason why he should not bring the driver into the planning of the work to be done in the few seconds the car is stationary.

179

In long-distance racing when a car stops at the pits for a change of drivers, it is interesting to watch the performances of the driver coming off duty and the one going on (33). The tired and dirty driver who has just finished is usually somewhat deafened by three hours' driving and will insist on shouting at the top of his voice into his team-mate's ear, and the new driver is often so keyed-up, especially if the car is leading, that he is not very receptive to rather incoherent shouting; the result is often a waste of time as far as imparting information goes. Some drivers will come in, climb on to the pit counter and merely say "It's O.K." and leave it at that; another will come in and say, "There are no brakes, the steering is pulling to the left, mind the oil on the Ess-bend, and the crashed car at the end of the straight, and don't go over 6,000 r.p.m. I think the bearings are going, and the mist is bad by the bridge; there's a funny noise in third so don't use it too much, and the road is as slippery as hell"—all in one breath amid the turmoil of passing cars and loudspeakers. The new driver about to take over then starts off in a complete whirl of information, most of which he didn't really hear properly and he spends the first half-hour creeping along trying to remember everything his co-driver has told him. One of the most expressive drivers in a pit-stop is Duncan Hamilton, especially at Le Mans, and I shall never forget one change-over in the Jaguar pit at night in teeming rain. Duncan got out of the D-type, blew a stream of water from his mouth, and said to Tony Rolt, "It's bloody murder, old boy", and left it at that. I thought at the time that he could not have summed up the situation more accurately if he had talked for an hour.

Some of the best driver-change conversation takes place when you get two drivers of different nationality, such as Gonzalez and Trintignant when they drove for Ferrari at Le Mans, or Behra and Moss, or Fangio and Kling. In such cases there is no common language and communication is usually made by single-syllable words in some intermediate language such as Italian, or more often than not by simple hand signs, the operative indications being "good", "bad",

33 A change of drivers during a twenty-four-hour race is also the time for doing
a great deal of servicing on the car, and the mechanics and team-manager have
little time to spare for the drivers. In this Jaguar pit-stop at Le Mans,
"Lofty" England is keeping a close watch on the hard-working mechanics,
while Tony Rolt, who has just finished three hours driving, is telling Duncan
Hamilton "all about it"—though Duncan looks as though he would prefer to
find out for himself

34 There is nothing like winning a race to boost up the morale of the team. Here Fangio is seen after winning the French Grand Prix for Mercedes-Benz, surrounded by an excited and happy group, including two of his mechanics helping him from the cockpit. In the background, also enjoying Fangio's victory are Mike Hawthorn and the late Onofre Marimon

35 Because of the qualities required to drive a racing car to its limit and to win races, the racing driver is essentially a character out of the ordinary run of human beings and is amusing company. This group before the start of a Grand Prix shows a number of them, in a fairly serious mood, with nothing in common other than the ability to drive fast. *Left to right:* Hawthorn, Salvadori, Brooks, Bonnier, Trintignant, Behra and the late Luigi Musso, representing Britain, Sweden, France and Italy

"so, so" or "hopeless". In such cases driver communications are short and to the point, but where both drivers are of the same nationality there tends towards too much talk and confusion.

In Grand Prix racing pit-stops are usually much shorter and there is little time for talk, while driver changes are not normal, but even so there are a few drivers that I consider behave impeccably during a pit-stop. The real test comes when the car has trouble and they have to make a stop that is not scheduled, or when something goes wrong during a routine stop. Of all the drivers Fangio stands out as the perfect example in such cases, and two races will live for ever in my memory. One was the Belgian Grand Prix in 1951 when he was leading in an Alfa Romeo and stopped for a routine refuel and a change of rear wheels. Everything was going with its usual split-second accuracy until the mechanic tried to remove the near-side rear wheel and it jammed. The rear wheels were new experimental ones and a spoke had broken and jammed the wheel on to the splined hub. When a pit-stop is being measured in seconds the first refusal of the wheel to slide easily off the hub was the signal for alarm, and Fangio took one look and then walked quietly away and stood by the pit counter. Within twenty seconds it became obvious that the wheel was not going to come off and some improvisation was going to be needed, while all Fangio's precious lead had gone and the second man had already gone by. The mechanics did a wonderful piece of work removing the whole hub and brake drum from the axle shaft, taking it behind the pit, removing the tyre and tube, fitting new ones and then refitting the complete assembly to the hub shaft, including tightening and split-pinning the hub nut. The whole operation took nearly fifteen minutes and meanwhile Fangio sat quietly on the pit counter, saying nothing to anyone, for all those in the pit were in a high old state of flap, or else they were working. Throughout the whole incident his face showed not the slightest trace of emotion, and whereas he might well have been in a raging temper at having his first place snatched from him like that, or been black with pent-up emotions, he showed not the slightest sign. The pit-staff had more than enough to deal with and afterwards must have been truly thankful that they did not have a highly-strung excitable driver in their midst as well. When the job was finished Fangio got swiftly into the car and was off again as though the whole thing had been planned, but all hope of catching the leader was now gone for ever. Needless to say he drove faster than ever after that stop.

The other occasion was at Pau when he was driving a 4CLT Maserati and stopped to refuel. It was in the early days of his "Scuderia Achille Varzi" and they did not have an electric starter for the car, instead a mechanic inserted a starting handle and wound away. No signs of life came from the engine, and as the first mechanic became exhausted another took over, and then two of them wound the handle together, but nothing happened. The car would not start. All this time Fangio was sitting impassively at the wheel, until finally he could stand it no more and he jumped out, politely but firmly moved the mechanics to one side, and gave the handle a sharp pull upwards, at which the engine burst into life. He leaped back into the cockpit and drove back into the race, leaving a weary pit-staff behind him. What had been happening was that the mechanics were winding the engine round, starting on the downwards swing of the handle, so that though they wound it round and round they were not reaching the same crankshaft speed at the point of the magneto firing as a sharp pull *upwards* just on the firing point provided. Realising this, Fangio thought it better to try himself and see if that was the trouble rather than try and shout an explanation from the cockpit.

When drivers come into the pits there are often amusing incidents, and one of the funniest is when a driver has been out practising in a very noisy car and not been wearing ear-plugs. He arrives back somewhat deafened and proceeds to talk in a very loud voice that can be heard three or four pits distant. Normally this doesn't matter much, but quite often the driver has some pretty voluble things to say about the car, other drivers or the circuit, and if at that moment the pits should be comparatively quiet the silence is broken by a stream of invective in a very loud voice. Attempts to quieten him down usually cause more chaos, for his friends tell him not to shout so loud, using a normal tone, which of course, he cannot hear, and often thinking they didn't understand he repeats himself only louder, for to his deafened ears his voice sounds quite normal. At such times it is best merely to go away.

There are many other ways in which a driver can hinder or help his team when he is not actually winning races for them, and one day at Monza I was watching the Scuderia Maserati carry out some testing, killing two birds with one stone by trying out their latest 2-litre four-cylinder sports car and at the same time letting promising Italian drivers have a test on this "works" car. There were four or five Italians present, all of whom owned Maserati sports cars and who had done a fair bit of racing, and as the big Supercortemaggiore race was due to take place team-manager Ugolini was on the lookout for some drivers to put in the "works" team. Among those having a try were Bellucci, Scarlatti, Piotti and Boffa, all experienced in small-time national sports-car racing, but having their first try with a good factory car. Much work had gone into the new 200S sports car and it was reckoned to be a lot faster than the contemporary 2-litre Ferrari, so that Maserati had put all their faith in the car to win the Supercortemaggiore race. They were testing on the road circuit at Monza, and it was known that the 2-litre Ferrari was lapping at just on two minutes, so it was hoped that the 2-litre Maserati would get below this figure. All the private-owners were given a try but the times were depressingly slow, the best being around 2 minutes 10 seconds, while most of them were nearer 2 minutes 15 seconds. As each driver had a try and the times did not improve, the chief engineer and the head mechanic were becoming very depressed, for on such a simple circuit as Monza they could not believe that drivers could make a difference of more than 10 seconds. With a longer and longer face Bertocchi, the head mechanic, kept putting up the lap times on a board as each driver went by the pits, but Bellucci was the only one who could consistently approach 2 minutes 10 seconds, and every time the car came in the mechanics looked at the plugs, checked the carburation and ignition, while Alfieri rechecked that the rear-axle ratio and tyre size were right, and all the time everything was in order. Ugolini was getting depressed just reading his stop-watch, and the air around the pits was one of great unhappiness. The Italians show displeasure or animation in a much more vigorous manner than the British or Germans for example, and when an Italian team is depressed it can be felt by everyone.

After a while Perdisa arrived, and being an up-and-coming lad, especially on sports cars at that time, he was quickly put in the 2-litre and sent off round the track. The result was only slightly better, his times being around 2 minutes 9 seconds, the only real improvement being that he was consistent.

Stirling Moss was due to arrive, but was a bit late having flown in from England, and by the time he arrived everyone was thoroughly miserable and a bit irked at him being late, so that no one was inclined to talk to him in English or French, which is always a bad sign with the Maserati team; it means things are not going well. Rather begrudgingly the mechanics checked the fuel, oil and tyres, and Moss got in, but everyone was convinced that it was a waste of time and that the new 2-litre just was not good enough. What was worse was that the race was only a few days off and it was too late to do much about the car, while the existing six-cylinder models were outclassed by the new Ferrari. Moss did a lap to get the feel of the car and then turned one in 2 minutes 7 seconds, whereupon a bit more interest was taken. Then he did 2 minutes 5 seconds and followed it with a succession of laps in 2 minutes 3 seconds. Now the atmosphere really began to change, and when a little later he clocked 2 minutes 1 second Bertocchi could not get the numbers on the signalling board quick enough. By the time Moss had got down to 2 minutes and two-fifths of a second, Alfieri was beginning to smile, and then when Ugolini announced a lap in 1 minute 59 seconds everyone was dancing about with glee, and Bertocchi was holding the board way above his head and grinning all over his face. Moss finally reached a fantastic 1 minute 58 seconds and the whole team were bubbling with enthusiasm; from the chief engineer down to the truck driver, they were all about three feet off the ground, and all the gloom of the rest of the afternoon had disappeared. When Moss eventually stopped and praised the car loudly I don't think I have ever seen such a happy and relieved group of people. Bertocchi actually kissed Stirling on the cheek, and everyone wanted to shake his hand, while the mechanic wiped the car down and checked the fuel and oil like a mother looking after her baby. The jubilation was not because they thought Moss was a wonderful driver, it was because he had renewed their faith, not only in the new car but also in themselves. When they arrived they had been so certain that the new car was good that they had a childlike faith in their belief, and when none of the lesser drivers could make it go fast they just could not believe that they had made a mistake and were wrong. It is this wide difference in moods that the Italians have, and show with great feeling, that makes them so pleasant to work with. I don't think that Moss really appreciated just how much he did for the Maserati people that afternoon, for he was not able to witness the joy which spread over the gloomy faces as they realised that their new car was a success after all. The top drivers in any team can bring about this uplifting of morale without realising it, for it usually happens while they are out driving, but it is a very important facet of a great driver. Fangio is one of the greatest morale boosters of all time, and his mere presence can keep a team going when they would normally lose heart (34).

It is fitting to record that after the episode with the new 2-litre Maserati the team went home convinced that they could win the all-important Supercortemaggiore, but on the first day of official practice they were plunged into the depths of gloom from which they did not recover until after the race.

Still looking for a suitable driving partner for Moss, Ugolini let Farina try the car and, on the very first lap, he went too fast into a corner and crashed the car beyond repair. Moss was very peeved about this, as can be imagined, but his feelings were nothing compared with those of the engineers and mechanics who had built the car.

In the 1957 Mille Miglia our $4\frac{1}{2}$-litre Maserati was going like a bomb, and we were really convinced that we could win the race, not only beating the whole Ferrari team, but we reckoned we could beat the record speed we had set up in the Mercedes-Benz in 1955. Conditions were perfect and we both felt on top of our form when we left the start. Imagine our feelings when the car broke down only seven miles from the start, as previously described. When we returned to the garage we were boiling with rage and prepared to start a fight with everyone in the Scuderia Maserati. As we drove the car into the garage the faces of all the mechanics and the team manager were almost beyond description; they were as a group of children who had just been told that there was no Father Christmas—they just did not believe their eyes—while some of them were genuinely in tears and beyond even expressing sympathy. When Ugolini heard that the brake pedal had broken off at the root he went a grey colour and became speechless and overcome with emotion. I have seen him lose his temper many times, and go from red to purple, but grey I had never seen. Stirling and I were so affected by the emotions of the rest of the team that we were quite unable to lose our tempers with anyone, and I recall Stirling saying something to the effect of the whole incident being a pity, but perhaps we could win it next year. He showed remarkable self-control, and I know that everyone in that little group in the garage not only respected him more than ever but were truly heartbroken for him. Whereas most British people would have said something like "damn bad luck", the Italian mechanics, with looks on their faces almost of dead people, shook hands with us with such feeling that I have never before experienced, and said nothing at all. There was nothing to say; it was written all over their faces; mere words could not do justice to what they were feeling at that moment. The following week I was down at Modena and everywhere this remarkable expression of sympathy, unspoken but oh how moving, was shown by all the workers at the factory. The more intimate ones came up and offered a handshake, with no spoken word but with an immense amount of true feeling. Personally I like the Italians, they are a funny, noisy crowd of people, wild and unpredictable, but with a simple sincerity that is hard to appreciate until you have been on the receiving end of it. While the failure of the car was an enormous disappointment to me, I am glad now that I was able to have the experience of the true sympathy of the Italians.

CHAPTER XV

RETIREMENT

PROVIDING our racing driver has managed to avoid serious accidents and has developed sufficient of the necessary qualities to become one of the top few, the day must arrive when he has to make a decision about retiring. To a driver who has had a successful career and climbed to the top of the tree, this is the most difficult decision he has to make, and many are the instances over the years of the right and wrong ways of ending a successful racing career. It is a sad thing that many great drivers end their careers prematurely in a serious accident resulting in permanent injury or death, but let us concern ourselves with those who retire sound in wind and limb.

When a young driver is showing great ability and beginning to climb to the top, it is obvious that he is going to replace one of the drivers already at the top and, as the pinnacle is being the World Champion, you can see that it is not an enviable position, nor an easy one to maintain. All your rivals are trying their utmost to drag you down off that pinnacle in order that they may take your place and, as time goes on, it becomes very obvious who your immediate successors are likely to be. There are two alternatives: one is to fight to retain your position at the top until you are defeated; the other is to step down and hand over the pinnacle gracefully to someone who is the obvious successor to the title of "the best". If you choose the first path it requires enormous personality and character to carry off successfully, for once one of the younger up-and-coming drivers has a fingerhold on the pinnacle he will pull the reigning champion down remorselessly. When that happens, and the downward path is started, there are many more hands and feet that will assist the fall. No one striving to reach the top is going to pause to assist a fallen star, for it is not a natural human instinct in personal competition. As I have said, great personal charm and character can allay this trampling under by the rush of new-blood ascending the ladder, but it does not often happen. Villoresi is a good example of a driver who was at the top and who climbed down gracefully, acknowledging the superiority of the new drivers who were replacing him. In 1954 in the Italian Grand Prix he drove fantastically fast in a Maserati, and again in the Supercortemaggiore sports car race in 1955 he drove splendidly in a small OSCA, and they were his last real efforts before retiring, so that people remember Luigi with affection, saying, "The old boy could still have a go right to the end of his career." On the other hand there are drivers who refuse to give up and get slower and slower until they become a laughing stock. People say of them, "Oh yes, he could drive twenty years ago, but he is making a pathetic exhibition of himself now."

Philippe Etancelin retired in the right manner; he gave up when he felt he was too old to do justice to the cars, but in the last two years came out of retirement to drive at Rouen, as he lives on the edge of the circuit and it was "just for old time's sake". When Eric Oliver was the reigning sidecar champion he always used to say he would retire when there was another rider on the starting grid whom he knew he could not beat. Although many people will not agree with me, I believe that he never saw that other rider on the starting line. He eventually retired because old age was beginning to affect the very high standard of his faculties. The spirit was always in him to lead the race from the fall of the flag, but in 1955 Sidecar T.T. he let his most dangerous rival take the lead and set the pace. The result was that a stone got flung into his passenger's face and he was forced to stop. That made him realise it was time to retire, for if he no longer had the will to go straight out in front he was no longer racing seriously, so he thought it best to stop before

191

he began to relax on other important factors. He retired from racing leaving the knowledge behind him that he had never been consistently beaten and seldom, if ever, out-ridden, and though there may be sidecar riders that are better than Oliver, few people are going to allow it to be admitted. The same feeling applies to Fangio in Grand Prix racing; having retired, his name will live on as a house-hold word representing genius with a racing car.

One of the finest retirements in the motor-cycle world was that of Freddie Frith, a charming, quiet and retiring character who won every World Championship 350-c.c. race in 1949 by sheer brilliance of riding ability and who, at the end of the season, hung up his leathers and said, "That's the finish, I've now retired", and he never rode a racing motor-cycle again. Harold Daniell stepped down from the top and handed the number one position in the Norton team to Geoff Duke, and he did it with such wit and charm that Geoff was never tempted to take advantage of his superiority over his team-leader. In 1950 when Daniell retired he still had an enormous number of followers who rated him a real World Champion rider. When it became obvious that Duke was heading for stardom, Daniell accepted the fact with pleasant wit. Even though he finished ahead of Duke he would say afterwards, "I must give this up, the young 'uns are making me go too fast." When he was finally beaten by Duke on sheer ability he retired from racing, but he lived on in the affections of the followers of the sport for being a true sportsman. It is easy to see the effect that the stars leave behind them, for of one man people will always say, "In his day there was no one to touch him, and he could still give some of the lads a run for their money now." Of another you will hear, "Maybe he was good in his day, but that was a long time ago and times change."

Having finally retired what does the racing driver do? If he has been a professional and put everything he has into his racing activities it has usually been at the expense of developing any other ability, so that though he may be only forty to forty-five years old, he is not mentally fitted to start any sort of work, and unless he has amassed a fortune in his short racing life he can hardly retire completely—and there are no pensions in motor racing. Most of the drivers develop some sort of business while they are racing, usually connected with the motor trade or the motor industry, and in that way they can profit from their success in the motoring sphere. Usually anyone who races to such an extent that it becomes a way of life cannot give up completely and, though they may stop driving, few of them leave the game altogether. After all, it is only reasonable that if you spend ten or twenty years extracting enjoyment and profit from the racing game, when you stop racing you should try and put something back into racing for the benefit of the newcomers. Take a typical British race meeting, at Silverstone for example, organised by the British Racing Drivers' Club; there you will find that most of the officials are old racing men, not necessarily well-known Grand Prix drivers of the past, but at some time or other they took an active part in competitions. These men are all enthusiasts for motor racing, probably from early childhood most of them, and after competing as much as they could manage they now give back to the sport some of the fun they took out of it—by helping to run meetings for today's drivers. If we look through a Silverstone programme the first obvious thing is that the Secretary of the B.R.D.C. was himself an active clubman in pre-war times, competing regularly in rallies, speed trials and small race meetings, while the President needs no introduction, almost any race report during the 1930's contained the name of Lord Howe, driving Maserati, Bugatti, E.R.A. and Lagonda cars to name but a few. But let us look down the list in the front of a typical programme, not so much at the figureheads running the meeting, but at the multitude of marshals and observers. Names such as R. J. W. Appleton, L. P. Driscoll, A. P. R. Rolt, K. D. Evans, J. H. T. Smith, R. King-Clarke, M. Morris-Goodall are some who were well-known competitors not so very many years ago. There is exactly the same situation on the continent. In Italy, for example, names of retired racing drivers continue to figure in race meetings on the organising side; names such as those of Villoresi, Lurani, Cornaggia, Sterzi, Brivio are all people who took a lot of fun out of motor racing and now that they are retired are prepared to put back into the sport a great deal of work and responsibility in order that today's drivers may enjoy the same amount of fun.

Naturally not all retired racing drivers help on the organising side, for some of them take on full-time jobs connected with the trade side of motor racing, or with active teams— and this is just as commendable—for it shows a true love of the sport of motor racing. When Reg Parnell retired from the Aston Martin team it was not a bit surprising that he took over the job of team-manager, for who would be better qualified to deal with the complicated task of understanding team management, or for that matter dealing with drivers, than one of the drivers themselves? I always derive a great deal of satisfaction when I see this sort of thing happen, and surely a new driver is given far more confidence and encouragement when he comes under the control of a man like Parnell whose exploits with Aston Martin, B.R.M., Ferrari and Maserati are legion. I well remember a day at Goodwood when some "recruits" were being given a try-out on a DB3S at Goodwood under Parnell's eagle eye, and it was a delight to listen to his instructions to the pupils; no flowery impressive language, but straight talk, which you knew the young drivers would listen to, for they had watched Parnell "dicing" at Goodwood not so long ago. One of them was taken round the circuit by Parnell in a DB2 saloon by way of an introduction, and when they returned the "recruit" said to me, "By golly, the old —— really knows his way round, it was quite an experience." When drivers can say that of their team-manager it must surely be a good thing, and when the team-manager was one of the drivers a few years ago it is surely an obvious thing.

A similar case is with Mercedes-Benz for, back in the 1920's when Alfred Neubauer became team-manager, he came from being a competitor himself, and now that he is retired Karl Kling has taken his job, and while Kling may not have proved himself the equal of Moss and Fangio in the classic year of 1955, no one will question Kling's driving ability, especially with a 300SL; remember his second place in the 1952 Mille Miglia in the pouring rain? Unfortunately there are not so many retired racing drivers with the necessary requirements, or for that matter the opportunities, to become team-managers, but any that do so are making one of the most valuable contributions possible to the sport.

Quite a lot of drivers, even when they are competing in full-time racing, have their own commercial firms, and naturally retirement means that they turn their attention to their business, for more than likely it has suffered a bit while they took time off to race. Today, for example, World Champion Mike Hawthorn has a flourishing motor business in Farnham, and when the day comes and he retires from active competition, he will be kept pretty busy with his business affairs, but there is little doubt that he will still be around the circuits, helping as marshal or observer. Truly professional drivers, who rely on their income from motor racing as their sole means of support, are few and far between; in fact I doubt whether a single one exists, for if not connected with the motor trade or industry, all racing drivers have some other business in the background, whether it be farming like Peter Walker, or television contracts like Stirling Moss. When you look around the motor trade, either at second-hand dealers, or agents for new cars, it is amazing how many well-known names are hidden behind business styles. At Tolworth Motors, for example, you find Roy Salvadori is the leading light; at H. W. Motors of Walton you find George Abecassis; Bueb at Cheltenham; at Blakes of Liverpool is Jackie Reece, and so on; while others prefer to use their own names, such as V. W. Derrington or J. H. Bartlett. Even in the industry, which to some people appears to contain nothing but business men who know little of competitions, you find retired racing drivers—T. V. Selby at Bristols, Norman Garrad at Rootes, Marcus Chambers at B.M.C., the Aldingtons at A.F.N. Ltd.; it really is amazing when it is all added up just how much motor racing activity controls the fortunes of the British motoring world. Everywhere you turn you see instances of people, now on the administrative side, who have once been competitors, some in small club meetings, others in top-line Grands Prix.

At Utah in 1957 when M.G. broke world records, much of the organisation was laid on by Capt. G. E. T. Eyston, whose record-breaking accomplishments are almost legendary. He now plays a very big part in Castrol activities, while in France the Castrol representative is none other than Albert Divo, a well-known Grand Prix driver of the 1920's. For a long time Shell racing affairs were looked after by Jimmy Simpson, the crack T.T. motor-cycle rider, and on the staff of Esso is Geoff Murdoch, a regular T.T. rider for many years. Klenk, famous for his Mercedes-Benz and Alfa Romeo partnerships with Karl Kling, is competition manager of Continental Tyres—and so one can go on; every way you turn you find ex-racing drivers behind the scenes. I know full well that many of them take jobs connected with motor racing simply because they are not suited to anything else, having devoted so much time to racing at the expense of other interests, so that when they retire the only thing they "know" is racing. But apart from that I am quite convinced that there is a more underlying reason, and that is their deep love of the sport. Once a person gets bitten by the competition "bug" it is awfully difficult to shake it off, and even if they are strong-willed enough to give up active participation they still have the feeling for it, as is shown by their enthusiasm when working behind the scenes. I cannot imagine anyone working at a job connected with racing sticking to fixed hours, or not "talking shop" when away from the office or workshop. They all love racing far too much, and this feeling breeds a wonderful fellowship which spreads over the whole of the activities of motoring competitions, whether with two, three or four wheels; the basic force behind the interest is the same, and it is not confined only to Great Britain; no matter to what country you go you will find the same underlying sentiments and reasons for motoring sport.

Returning to our Grand Prix driver, the future is a matter he often has to contemplate—the future in the form of retirement that is—and occasionally I hear among the professionals remarks to the effect that when they retire they are going to get out of it all and have nothing more to do with motor racing or motor-cars; take up boating, or flying or something else, they say. First of all I doubt whether many of them will be capable of giving up their interest in motor racing as easily as that, for when you have made something in your life more than just an interest, between the ages of twenty and forty years, it is hard to break away from it. There is the possibility that they will make enough money to retire at an early age, but even so they will still need some outlet for their mental and physical energies and it is unlikely that they will find a new way of life quite so satisfying as that which they lived in motor racing. Apart from all this I am rather rude when I hear such a suggestion made, for in top-line racing these days drivers are taking out more than ever before, both financially and in enjoyment and experience. There is more money in motor racing these days—more motor racing anyway; the field of activities has spread over most of the world, giving opportunities to visit not only the whole of Western Europe, but the Americas and the southern hemisphere, and today's racing driver can take an enormous amount out of motor racing. Any such selfish suggestion that when they are finished they are going away from it all, makes me very sour, for I feel the least they can do is to try and put back some of that which they have taken out. It is only this ploughing back of the profits of enjoyment and experience over the years that keeps racing such a pleasant and sound pastime, and if everyone "takes" and never "gives" then the future will be very sad. Fortunately, as I have already shown, it will not happen, but any drivers who are selfish enough to contemplate such a move earn my disrespect very quickly, no matter how good they have been as drivers.

By means of this attitude of "giving something back to racing", the motor-cycle world is in a far healthier state than the car world, for amongst the two-wheeler lads a vast number join the motor-cycle trade, dealing in new and second-hand machines, even while they are racing themselves. Because of this their businesses often flourish, especially if they become successful riders, for the average motor-cyclist if he is buying a new Triumph or Norton gets satisfaction from buying it through an agent who has just won a T.T., rather than from an agent who doesn't even know what a T.T. is. When these riders retire, and build up their businesses into strong concerns, many of them will finance an up-and-coming rider and enter him for the big races, often supplying machines, mechanics and transport, as well as paying expenses. One can say that the ex-rider turned businessman is gaining by free advertising, especially if his *protégé* wins or does well, which is true, but it means laying out over £1,000 for somebody else to reap the enjoyment, or so it would seem. In actual fact the retired rider gets just as much enjoyment as the newcomer who is being supported, for it keeps him right in the thick of the game, and some men, fortunately, will never grow up. Their love is racing, and they like to stay in right to the end, even if it only means being the owner of a winning machine. Naturally such actions are not taken solely for sentimental reasons; they are handled with a certain amount of business acumen, but I do insist that the underlying reason why so many retired racing motor-cyclists continue to support up-and-coming youngsters is their true love of racing. This sort of thing does happen to a small extent in motor-car racing, but nothing like as much as in the motor-cycle world, which is a pity, and it is one of the reasons why I always feel that the spirit of comradeship in motor-cycling is much stronger than in motoring. It is probably closely tied up with some of the psychological reasons why people race at all, which I have dealt with already, but none the less anyone who has experience behind the scenes in motor-car and motor-cycle racing will, I think, agree that it is so.

This may be "preaching" but I cannot help that. I say that racing is fundamentally a pastime for the human being, something to occupy his mind and muscles over a certain part of his life span. It is not a natural activity, it is purely man-made and invented by man for the benefit of man, and that it has been kept alive and healthy because one of the unwritten rules has been: "Take as much as you can while you can, but afterwards—give some of it back." We shall always have people of a philanthropic frame of mind who will give back far more than they ever took out, though to many the act of giving is satisfaction in itself, so that "giving" is still "taking". One such man whom we have with us at present is Tony Vandervell, and his contribution to the game of racing, his team of Manufacturer's-Championship-winning Vanwall cars, is magnificent. Of course, all the time he is giving us the Vanwall team to win Grand Prix races he is getting enormous personal satisfaction, but the underlying reason for it all is his deep love of the racing game. There are thousands like him, but unhappily not so many who are able to stay in it in such a lavish and satisfying way.

Although the racing driver has a busy and complex life, especially while he is at the top as we have found out, at no matter what age he stops racing there is no need—in fact, there is no justification—for him to drop his activities: he merely has to redirect them. His natural instincts should do the rest.

INDEX

INDEX

The numerals in HEAVY TYPE refer to the *figure numbers*
of illustrations

Chambers, Marcus, 195
Chapman, Colin, 60, 94: **9**
Circuit, learning the, 47
Citroen DS19, 143
Clearways Bend, Brands Hatch, 153
Collins, Peter, 31, 33, 37, 52, 53, 66, 69, 80, 161: **12, 13**
Connaught, 47, 49, 56, 139, 175
  instrument panel on, **10**
Cornaggia, G., 194
Cornering, fast, 38, 41, 130, 149 *et seq.*: **1, 4, 28, 29, 31**
  forces acting on a wheel when, 140: **25, 26**
  limits, discovering, 87
Crystal Palace Circuit, 146
Cunningham, 92

Daimler-Benz, 63
Daniell, Harold, 192
De Dion rear suspension, 167
Derrington, V. W., 195
Determination, 29
  see also "Tigering"
"Dicing with Death", 43
Differential, restricted-slip, 159
Divo, Albert, 196
Dixon, Fred, 94
D.K.W., 143
Driscoll, L. P., 193
Drivers, mechanically expert, 59
  troublesome, 54 *et seq.*
Driving as an Art, Chap. I
  position on speed, effect of, 22
Duke, Geoff., 192

England, "Lofty", 33
E.R.A., 193
Etancelin, Philippe, 191
Evaluation of ability, self-, 34
Evans, K. D., 193
Eyesight, racing drivers' exceptional, 123
Eyston, Capt. G. E. T., 196

Fangio, Juan Manuel, 14, 31, 36, 38, 41, 50, 52, 54, 59, 70, 79, 80, 89, 90, 117, 120, 122, 126, 161, 173, 180, 183, 187: **12, 15, 21, 32, 34**

Fangio cornering with the 250F Maserati, 161, 162: **1**
Farina, Dr. Giuseppe, 38, 90, 117, 118, 188: **16**
Ferrari, 37, 79, 98, 118: **19**
  4-cylinder, 71
  4·5-litre, 38, 124: **5**
  Lancia-, 53, 66, 162: **13**
  "Monza", 90
  pedal lay-out, 169
  Scuderia, 53, 69
  steering-box, 54
  "Super-Squalo", 138, 161
Fitch, John, 33, 92
Flag, jumping the, 69, 71; **14**
  starting by, 69, 71
Ford, 138
Fordwater, Goodwood, 138, 146
Formula II, 167
Frazer-Nash, 131
French Grand Prix, 79: **12, 14, 34**
Frère, Paul, 90, 126
Fright, Chap. VIII, 178
Frith, Freddie, 192
Front-wheel drive, 143
"Full noise" (throttle), 75

Gabriel, Fernand, 14
Garrad, Norman, 195
Gearboxes, 168
Gedinne, 72
Gendebien, Olivier, 31, 33
Gerard, F. R., 126
Gilera, 65
Godia, 66
Gonzalez, José Froilan, 38, 111, 180: **5, 16**
Goodwood, 73, 194
  Fordwater Curve, 138, 146
  Madgwick Corner, **6**
Gordini, **15**
Gould, Horace, 66: **13**
Grand Prix driving, 14, 26–28, 31, 32
Gregory, Masten, 52, 66, 126: **18**
"Gull-wing" doors, 91
Guzzi team, 62